JO MAY

A Barge at Large II

Looking back, moving on

Copyright © 2021 by Jo May

All rights reserved. No part of this publication may be reproduced, stored or transmitted in any form or by any means, electronic, mechanical, photocopying, recording, scanning, or otherwise without written permission from the publisher. It is illegal to copy this book, post it to a website, or distribute it by any other means without permission.

Jo May has no responsibility for the persistence or accuracy of URLs for external or third-party Internet Websites referred to in this publication and does not guarantee that any content on such Websites is, or will remain, accurate or appropriate.

First edition

*This book was professionally typeset on Reedsy.
Find out more at reedsy.com*

To Maggie

Thank you

Contents

Heading North	1
Why?	7
Canal des Vosges	17
Loto!	24
St. Jean Reflections	30
Where did you start?	36
End of an Era	44
Peniche Aster - Magnifique	51
New Loo and a Road Trip	70
Riqueval Tunnel	84
BIG Canals	89
Dunkirk and on to Belgium	94
New Horizons	100
First Look at our New Home	104
Diksmuide	109
Stop Thief	116
Motorhome (Wreck on wheels)	120
Shopping Woes	126
Uncle Percy	131
How to win Friends.....	135
Camper Battle	140
Back to Blighty	152
Time to go Home	160
Bonus Chapter 24	168
About the Author	178
Also by Jo May	180

Heading North

Part One

How many times have you sat on a camel?

Not many, I'll wager (unless you're a Tuareg of course).

For me, it's once. Jan and I took a 'last minute' trip to Israel and we came across an enterprising native offering camel rides. The beast in question was at rest, parked in the dust with its legs tangled up beneath it. I'm scared of heights so asked whether I could just sit on it as it was, and have my photo taken.

'Certainly,' said the keeper, 'that'll be 30 shekels.'

So, for roughly £5 I am immortalised on celluloid. Or would have been if Jan hadn't missed my head off the photo. This was in the days before digital photography so it was with some excitement that I visited the chemist to reclaim my photos. The snapshot I was eager to see depicted a patch of dusty camel park, the camel (with a patient facial expression) and me – up to shoulder level.

'Well, I was focussing on the camel,' said Jan. 'We've already got plenty of you.'

Talk about getting the hump.

This little episode is an example of an emotional balloon deflating. It's like setting off on a cruise and the engine fails to start. Store cupboards are stocked with tinned stuff, farewells bid and routes planned – then you're let down by a lump of unwilling engine. Yep, this is what happened at the start of our 2014 trip. While waving goodbye to our mates there was a disappointing lack of noise as I pressed the starter button. Fortunately, I could put this right with a short scramble to the engine room to re-connect the starter battery. To get another camel shot would mean a further trip to Israel, and we haven't time (or money) – besides the camel has probably retired by now.

We set off from St. Jean de Losne, at the junction of the Canal de Bourgogne and the River Saone, in June – roughly two months later than planned. Why we even bother with a plan is a mystery, we should just fill up with food and diesel and set off when the mood takes us. Actually, we've never filled up with diesel – we simply can't afford it! The white diesel tank is 1,200 litres and we never have 1,600 Euros available all at one go – unless we do without food and dog biscuits for three months. No, we just dribble fuel in as and when we can.

We do know people who plan everything almost to the hour over a five or six month trip. They lay it all out on a spreadsheet - where they are stopping for lunch, where they'll moor for the night, in which town they'll stop six weeks hence etc. etc. This is too inflexible for us, if we find a nice spot we might stay a couple of days. We have been known to stop for three weeks – like we did in Lutzelboug on the Marne au Rhin Canal on the way east to Strasbourg.

We're heading north on River Saone towards the Canal des Vosges and there has been talk of a lack of water – canal restrictions, even closures. Water shortage? You've got to be joking. It's lashing down – has been for days. It's the wrong sort of rain apparently. We're getting heavy, lumpy stuff interspersed with the odd proper downpour. This type just runs straight off the hills into someone's garage – what we need is the persistent drizzly stuff that soaks in. So, we battle on, almost blind, wet through, waiting for the right kind of drizzle - waiting for the perfect storm.

The Saone is an extension of the River Rhone and is part of a route on which you can travel inland from the Mediterranean, via other canals and rivers all the way to northern Holland. The Vosges are a mountain range in Eastern France near the German border. Actually, when I investigate a bit I find that they're not really mountains at all – they are in fact the western edge of the unfinished Alsatian Graben. That sounds terrible so if anyone asks – they are mountains. To be frank they're not exactly Himalayan, more pimply, but they are scenic.

I've just given up smoking - ciggies anyway. I'm puffing away on an E-cig (cherry flavour allegedly, though it tastes like a budget hand-cleaner) but it's a month since I've had tobacco. I might look a bit of a plonker but it's a step in the right direction. It's cheaper too so with diesel to buy for the summer, giving up the fags has been a boost to the coughers!! See what I did there – with a bit of innocent wordplay I have turned a paragraph with a horrible subject into something worthy of a moderate hack. (Oh, did it again!).

Via Auxonne, Lamarche and Pontailler we spent 3 days in Gray in the company of three other boats from St. Jean. Actually, one of the guys here is the reason I'm puffing on a vapour tube. When I first saw him with one a couple of months ago I told him, quite candidly, that he looked a complete tosspot. Well, he now re-pays the compliment, with the addition of a few well-chosen adjectives.

If we're serious about maintaining our health we should avoid my BBQs. But we don't - and after a brief visit to hospital we set off again. The owners of these three boats are people we've become friends with over the past few years. Neil and Jan, Sandra and Richard and Pete with whom we have shared some fun. As we say cheerio we're not to know that a month hence we will make the decision not to return to St. Jean. It's peculiar, we have shared much over the previous five years, as we have with so many great folk in Burgundy, but we may never see them again. If I'd known that this may have been the last goodbye, would I have treated it any differently? No, I'd have been just as rude!

We're heading for Savoyeux to join our old friend Narrowboat Bob and his lovely French girlfriend Christianne - plus his dog Dozer, an English Bull Terrier who we first met when he was 8 months old. He was a substantial item then, now three years older he's even more substantial – but lovely natured, if strong. Though that didn't prevent Tache (our terrier / poodle cross) from biting his nose when Dozer got a bit too familiar with his rear end.

We've actually done all this stretch before, although in the opposite direction five years ago. Long-term boaters tell us that travelling in the opposite direction on a waterway offers a whole new perspective – for me it is the opportunity to re-visit things I collided with last time. Much Merlot has flowed under the bridge since we last passed so fortunately I can't remember most of it. But soon we head for undiscovered territory – namely a little place called Traves. It's up a 5 kilometre off-shoot at a place called Rupt, just before lock 8 on The Saone. There's a little sign that warns 'at own risk' – this is because it's shallow at times (like me). Bob had warned us that he'd got stuck up there, precisely at the entrance to the lake where the moorings are located. It wasn't marked by buoys when he did it so it's easy to see how he ran aground. He'd tried all sorts to get free – like emptying his water tank and revving like mad in both forward and reverse. He'd even got into the water and tried to shove the thing off but he finally had to call out International Rescue who towed him out.

We moored next to a paddock of six donkeys with their enthusiastic entourage of flies.

It's a pretty little area and we're moored right at the northern end of the lake. Away to the right is a cafe / restaurant with parasol-shaded seating (and wifi) to service the fifty or so holiday chalets and touring caravans and motor homes. It's peculiar because the place is deserted apart from us and one other boat. They are a French couple moored on one of the little wooden pontoons just along the bank. They went to the local restaurant for dinner. Celebrating their wedding anniversary, they had obviously had an aperitif before they set out and gave us a tiddly 'bon soir' as they passed. They'd definitely overdone it in the restaurant because on the way back the lady collapsed in a heap on the grass outside our boat. Undignified doesn't begin to describe it. He wasn't much better but he had to literally drag her backwards by the armpits 60 metres to their boat. Her heels left two parallel lines in the wet grass. She lay on the pontoon and it took him 30 minutes of cajoling and face-slapping before they attempted to board their boat. Fortunately, this was one of the evenings when I was only half pickled so, although it wasn't necessary, I could have helped if required.

That's an evening they won't remember in a hurry.

We often arrive in a place to find it's 'shops closed day'. Doesn't matter what day of the week it is, we seem to pick 'em. In Port sur Saone, a town of not inconsiderable size, there wasn't a shop at all – 'unless you wait 2 weeks till the new supermarket opens', said a local lady helpfully. But I did see a family of six kingfishers and a herd of deer on my morning walk. Not much good if you're starving but lovely to see nevertheless.

Also, here Jan becomes involved with a wedding. She tends to lurk around the fringes of these occasions and is often there so long that she's presumed part of the festivities. After all there are very few guests who will know everyone else. She doesn't go the wedding breakfast you understand, just mingles and sometimes follows everyone into the church. The Church bit is only for religious blessing anyway, the official ceremony happens in the town hall. There's usually plenty of standing around, folks in their wedding tackle gathered in the town square, smoking and chatting. Here in Port sur Saone, a very flimsy and temporary tiered scaffold has been erected. Guests, some of whom look neither nimble nor light, clamber up nervously and have their photos taken. The scaffold is right next to the canal and by-standers fear a major disaster – which thankfully doesn't materialize. We're not sure whether the vehicle parked nearby is the official 'off on honeymoon' one but there's a small white plumber's van parked under a 'WC Publics' sign. It's bedecked with balloons and two life-size guy Fawkes-type dummies, which presumably represent the happy couple. The dummies are awful things and could be baddies from a Tolkein novel. Anyhow, it looks like they're off on honeymoon in the van - perhaps he's got a job to go to en route – or she has. Let's not be sexist! Actually, she looked lovely in a lacy dress and he definitely looked like the plumber – wearing drainpipes!!

You have to be wary of advertising posters. Many are of historic interest but bear little relevance to anything today. People plaster them to lampposts, fences or buildings where they are left, sometimes for aeons, to degrade. Fine if you want to visit last years vide grenier (car boot sale), but generally not much good in the present. We arrive at Corre which is where the River Saone morphs into the Canal des Vosges. It was with a degree of scepticism that I went to verify the claim of free delivery from the nearby supermarket, one kilometre from our mooring.

'Oui. Bien sur' (Yes. Of course), said the lady on the till.

'Splendid', says I, 'I'll go and get a shopping list'.

I cycled back to the boat to retrieve the list. It turned out to be a bit of a monster - the skipper making full use of the supermarkets benevolence to stock up on 'heavy items'. So, I cycled back again and spent considerably more than 100 euros and told the lady on the till I was ready for the delivery. I met a nice chap outside who put our stuff in his van. Because there are alternative moorings, both on the canal and in the nearby marina just off the river, I was quite specific as to where we would like our goods delivered and I set off back on my bike to wait for him.

'Be with you toute suite' (imminently), he'd said.

Toute suite turned into half an hour, then an hour – so I thought I'd better go and investigate. I set off again on the bike. Now half way into my fifth kilometre I noticed a strange noise to the rear. I was being chased by the dog! He'd hopped off the boat and was following me down the road. After a brief delay while he chased a cat through a farmyard, I got him back to the boat and set off yet again for the supermarket. The delivery man was very honest actually. He told me he'd had a phone call after I'd left which became protracted, then he'd forgotten! This time he actually followed me down the road in his van (he could just about keep up) and finally the delivery was complete. Some of the stuff was now out of date, but mission accomplished. The energy I'd expended over seven speedy kilometres to and fro was considerable. So much so that I was probably in 'negative equity'. In other words, I needed to eat so much to replace the calories I'd burned that I needed to go shopping again.

While here in Corre I was talked at by a gregarious German chap. He'd asked me initially if I spoke his language. I obviously got 'no' wrong in German because he spent 30 minutes telling me of his voyage to date. At least that's what I presume he was telling me. I recognized the word 'Berlin' and 'Lyon', but the rest was lost in the mists. I'd smile and chuckle when he did – just to feel part of things – but, in addition to the initial 'nine', I only said 3 words throughout the exchange – alf veeder sane.

Why?

Many people have asked me why, or how, we ended up living on a boat. During our twenty something years together Jan and I have made two big changes. The first from Lancashire to Shropshire, the second from house to boat. Big upheavals both but driven by a need to get on with life after Jan's dire health prognosis in the mid-nineties. Of the two, house to boat was the most testing. We had to come to terms with a number of things. Could we forego the relative space and comforts of a house and the security of a reasonable job? Could we afford to do it?

But perhaps the more salient question was, could we afford not to do it?

So how did it all start? Well, I touched on it briefly in the other *'At Large'* books but recently came across a piece long forgotten. Our dear old dog, Bonny, had a dreadful start in life but she re-paid our faith in her a thousand times with loyalty and friendship. Just prior to moving onto our first narrowboat, before I started a spell writing for a canal magazine and long before the first book, she wrote the following, which sums things up pretty well.....

If mum had told me ten years ago that I'd be living in a steel box, the internal dimensions of which measured forty feet by six, I would have told her to seek help.

I had a topsy-turvy start but when I was adopted, aged two, I had a real chance in life for the first time. I had eight increasingly carefree years. Now things have come crashing down in a heap. Mum and dad have moved onto a narrowboat.

What on earth do they think they're doing? We had a perfectly good house. I had my own room, my own bed and a couple of acres to run about in. Now this!

I shouldn't be ungrateful. I had two spells in a rescue centre though, looking back, I hardly think it was my fault. On the first occasion I had been chasing bicycles – no one told me it was illegal, no one explained it could have been dangerous, no one said 'please don't do that'. No one said please at all in the early days. I was deemed to have behavioural problems. I was sectioned and sent to a rescue centre. Then I was sent to live with a couple who booted me out onto the street because they couldn't be bothered to organise kennels for me when they were going on holiday. I was rounded up and sent back again.

After a few months I was getting a bit of a complex. During my internments I'd seen others come in, frightened and timid. Within a short time they would disappear. I tried to kid myself that they were happy and being loved somewhere. Friends of mine would be led away. Sometimes by a family to a waiting car, sometimes away on a leash in a dreadful silence, an awful quiet that engulfed those of us left behind. Invariably, wherever they went, we would never see them again.

I know that our keepers tried to find us homes. People came and looked. Each time we brushed ourselves down and started our well-rehearsed displays. We yelped and wagged as if our lives depended on it. Time after time people came and went and time after time we would settle back in our concrete mausoleums. It was so difficult to build myself up – each time it became more difficult stage my play. The smile would no longer reach my eyes. Some of my friends got angry but that wasn't my way. I was just sad and afraid.

One day I was asleep. My energy wasted by the roller-coaster of hope and despair. I awoke to a tapping. My gaoler stood there with a man and woman. It was such a battle to move but I dragged myself to the bars. My ears drooped and, hard as I tried, my tail just would not move. He was a short chap with a moustache, and she a bespectacled, kindly looking lady. Then she smiled. It was a beautiful smile, so natural, so gentle. I was desperate to respond. The tip of my tail quivered and I prayed it was enough.

My gaoler told the strangers that I was called Bonny and that I was a collie / retriever cross. The three of them took me for a short walk on my lead in the exercise field. The gaoler left and I was alone with the strangers. They crouched down and stroked me. Then they spoke to me, and in their kindly voices I heard *the whisper of my future.*

They agreed to foster me and if we all got on together they would adopt me. I lived with them in their rented house and showed my gratitude by helping in the garden, digging up the flowerbeds and fertilizing the lawn. I was nervous when they went out and left me at first, howling the house down, but when I knew they were coming back, I settled. This house was part of a farm and full of mice. There were enormous fields where I ran and chased crows when dad and I went on long early-morning walks.

A year later Mum and Dad bought their own house. Eventually, after Dad had built it, I had my own room, the conservatory, with my own two-seater sofa. I had wonderful views and a large garden and wood to play in. Mum and Dad didn't have children so I suppose I was a bit spoilt. Actually, Mum had a daughter but she lived with her dad over 100 miles away. She came to visit every now and then and she was just as nice as mum – same smile.

Dad went out to work but I could see that he wasn't enjoying it. He would get ratty about the traffic jams and kept mumbling about what a waste of time it all was. Pushing paper from here to there, talking to people he came to distrust on the phone, never actually creating anything that would last. Mum just kept sympathising and finally said that if he was sick of what he was doing, he must make a change. 'Pack it in and start again' she'd said. I'm not sure he'd bargained for quite that drastic a step but it must have sowed a seed.

I used to sleep on my sofa but every now and then Dad would be away for a night or two so I would go and sleep on the floor next to Mum. When he was away she would go to bed with the telephone and a bread knife. I never did work that one out. Every time he came home he was increasingly flustered and would have a glass or two of red wine and grumble about a stiff back.

I knew that Mum had been really sick at one time. Dad and I used to sit and chat in the wood. On one occasion he told me that Mum was once so poorly that the doctor told her in 1996 that she would not live to see the new millennium. Well, she did. Dad would shed a tear there in the wood. I would sit close by him with my head on his leg as he tickled my ears.

I would laugh with Mum about what a grumpy little sod Dad had become. I had the feeling though that the time was right for a big change for both of them.

'Bonny', he said one day, 'how do you fancy living on a boat'? Well, I didn't even know what a boat was. I'm not sure the word 'on' was too encouraging as you normally live 'in' something, but I smiled anyway. I'd live anywhere as long as I was with them.

I could see that Mum & Dad were excited so I decided to be excited too. We went all over the country looking at second-hand boats but each time either or both of them grumbled about this or that. Nothing seemed ideal. I stayed in the car so didn't have a say. They agreed the only way to get what they really wanted was to build their own. They talked a lot, which was good to hear, and I felt for the first time in a long while they shared a common goal.

They decided to get someone to build the shell for them, to a stage where it was weatherproof, and they would take it from there. I suppose Dad was pretty practical when it came down to it but every job he tackled at home seemed to coincide with a salvo of appalling language. Mum was arty so if it ever got to that stage I'm sure she could make it look pretty.

I'd soon cottoned on to the fact that a boat floated on water but couldn't imagine how anyone could actually live on one – yes, 'live', that was the word Dad used – yikes!

I could feel we were progressing and one day we drove to a huge tin shed on an industrial park. We parked close to the enormous doors and Mum & Dad went inside. From the car all I could see initially was a cloud of smoke but when it began to clear a strange grey shape appeared out of the mist. I could only assume that this was the shell they had been harping on about. It has taken me a while to trust anyone but I do trust Mum & Dad. If Dad says it will float, then float it will. It really didn't look too impressive so I retreated to my land of dreams.

Over the next six months there were periods of great excitement not least of which was when Dad opened a bottle of wine to celebrate that fact that the boat had been 'dropped in the water'. I wasn't too keen on that phrase either but they didn't seem concerned.

Dad was still going to work dressed in a suit but went on from there to work on the boat. He often did not get home till late in the evening dressed in his gardening clothes and usually covered in dust.

I knew we were in for a major upheaval when a shifty chap in a poncy car came to assess the house for sale. I didn't trust this bloke one bit, fake smile, fancy haircut. I was used to Mum's compassionate smile and Dad's double-crowned tufts. I felt there'd be tears before we'd finished. Looking back, I took a dislike because he was disrupting our life and I couldn't believe the metal thing I'd seen months earlier would ever become a home.

As it turned out I was right about the agent. The ponce had overvalued the house and we engaged two other agents before accepting an offer.

I really found this period quite stressful and I got increasingly angry. Mum and Dad had to put up with strangers telling them what a state their house was in and what changes they would have to make to make it liveable. What tosh! It's who is in a house, not what. Most of these buggers could live in a palace and still not have a home. Anyhow there was nothing I could do except snarl at the unpleasant ones and nip the worst.

Despite all this, amazingly, everything worked out perfectly. Mum and Dad moved most of the contents out to storage and we completed the house sale the very day our boat was ready - July 4th – Independence Day. I had a final walk round our garden with Mum and Dad, said goodbye to my first real home - and we left.

I was excited but apprehensive. When we go out in the car they never tell me how far we are going so I just have to be patient. There was so much stuff crammed in I could barely see out at all. I knew we were driving through the countryside so was very surprised when we turned into a gate and I saw a floating village. A mass of brightly coloured boats parked side-by-side, nose-in, down a dozen or more steel avenues. The boats gently rocked and swung in the breeze; a slow-motion ballet performed by these huge, gentle creatures. It was calming and welcoming. I sniffed the air and I knew there were friends for me here.

We walked down an avenue marked 'Strictly Private' (which sounded important). 'Welcome to our new home Bonny', said Dad. It was blue – and big!

He unzipped the awning at the front and we stepped onto the deck. I would learn the technical terms for everything in due course after I'd had a really good poke around. Despite my misgivings I wanted to put on a good show so wagged and sniffed for all I was worth and I was dying to see inside.

Double doors opened onto the lounge, down a couple of big steps we were in.

As I am only short I knew that I was standing below the water line which felt mighty peculiar and the constant swaying had me in a bit of a tangle. But it looked fantastic. Mum and Dad were beaming and I knew they were proud of what they had achieved. It was a lovely summers day and when Mum opened a side door (that only came halfway down the wall for some reason) a warm breeze blew through the boat ruffling my coat.

It really was like a little house and immediately I spotted my special little bed. It was oval with raised sides and a cushioned bottom and near a radiator. I immediately went and sat in it to let Mum and Dad know that I too was happy with our new home. It wasn't exactly my own sofa but I know that they had made every effort for me so I smiled to put them at their ease.

Front to back it went lounge, kitchen, dining room, bathroom and bedroom.

Behind the bedroom were a couple of steps leading up to a pair of doors. He slid part of the roof back (with a terrible squeaking noise – he'd have to do something about that) and opened some doors onto the back garden. Dad said the engine was under the floor here – whatever that meant. There was only six feet of it before it disappeared into a huge lake. I can't say I was too impressed with this at all. This worrying development gave me the collywobbles for the first time.

Then it got worse. Dad pushed a little button, pressed a little lever forward and turned a key. I've never heard such a racket. The sound was coming from where he had said the engine was so I could only hope that someone would soon come and mend it. I may not be very tall but I have extremely good hearing so it probably sounded far worse for me than them. The vibration made my teeth rattle. I rushed back and curled up in my bed – I knew Dad would be angry because part of his boat wasn't working properly. It was much quieter here but the distant rumble didn't stop. After a couple of minutes, the rumble became a gentle grumble so I thought it safe to go and investigate.

Mum and Dad were standing in the back garden smiling. If they were happy now I couldn't wait till they got everything working properly.

Satisfied that the engine made enough racket, Dad turned it off.

The silence that followed was magical. Gradually I took in more and more sounds. Birds sung in the trees and hedges that surrounded our village, water lapped against our boat as we moved around, a group of ducks quacked, a dog barked and people were laughing. I hoped they weren't laughing at Dad's engine.

Mum and Dad were talking to a couple on the next boat. She was a giggly blonde woman and he was a tall chap with the whitest legs I have ever seen. He caught me staring and coughed so I looked away sheepishly. A dog appeared between the forest of legs. 'This is Kayla' said white legs. 'We adopted her from some friends who were going abroad. When they got her as a puppy she cost six hundred pounds and they were told that she was a German Shepherd – but she never quite got there'. I hoped this was a fertilization issue and not natural selection or I could see the breed's popularity waning. She looked a happy soul though. We were to become trusted and good friends.

Though Mum and Dad never really talked about their insecurities to anyone but themselves, I heard it all. They worried about the future and whether they had done the right thing and sometimes fussed about money. I used to give them a lick to tell them that everything would be all right and remind them of when Mum had been so ill and Dad was blowing into a paper bag. I just tried to be calm, act myself, hoping they would follow my lead.

I would have long talks with Kayla and discovered that Alan and Julie had just the same fears. We couldn't understand why they constantly compared themselves to other people and why they were bothered about what other people thought about them.

That first night the grown-ups got together and drunk wine and beer. They talked loudly then turned the music up so they talked even louder. Dad went to the toilet a lot. They laughed at silly stories and Kayla raised her eyebrows at me and I knew what she was thinking. They even laughed at stories that I had heard Dad tell many times before. (Although Mum only drunk cranberry juice but she got just as silly.) For some reason Julie threw some wine on the floor.

We went to bed much later than usual and the following day Dad took some pills and rubbed his head a lot. He didn't look very well and spent the rest of the day in a grump watching telly.

I am fourteen now. Sometimes a noise on television, a tone of voice or a particular sound takes me back to my early days and I crawl onto Mum's lap for a cuddle. She understands that lonely fear. Thankfully these are now conscious thoughts. My dreams are happy and I am chasing crows or squirrels or walking with Mum and

Dad.

Believe it or not, after a couple of weeks, Dad announced that he wasn't too happy with this boat and said he was going to build another – better this time. So, unbelievably, off he went to buy another shell! This was delivered a few weeks later and parked on pontoon immediately opposite our original boat. It was handy I'll give you that, he only had six feet to go to walk to work. He spent every single day for 8 months battling away until it was finally finished.

It was a different colour, this one dark green with yellow lines on it – somebody pointed out that it resembled one of Dad's packets of Golden Virginia – a comment he ignored. I have to say though that this was a big improvement on his first attempt. this one was a 'Trad' – which I learned was short for traditional. In effect we had a smaller back garden and the whole thing was rather sleeker.

Going into the lounge, a rich, mellow tongue and groove covered the roof and halfway down the walls to a point where they seemed to step out a few inches. I later learned that this step was called the gunwale. Below the gunwale the sides were flat and painted a deep green. Brass fittings were everywhere; lights, switches, plug sockets, curtain rails and ceiling vents. The floor was solid dark oak. In the right front corner was a fireplace with red, green and yellow tiles and a cast iron fire with a chimney going up through the roof. In the front left corner were oak cupboards. One large one for the television and smaller ones running down the side wall that held CD's, books and booze. There were two big leather armchairs on either side of the cabin, one a few feet in front of the other.

Attached to the lounge was the kitchen, separated two thirds of the way across the cabin by a counter above which was a fancy cupboard attached to the side wall and suspended from the ceiling. There was a silver pole sitting on the worktop below supporting the cupboard. It didn't look awfully safe so I gave it a wide berth. We had all the mod cons (and some new cons compared to our last house): fridge, cooker double sinks, microwave and a larder that slid in and out of a tall cupboard. Pale blue doors really made it feel like a different room to the lounge. There were lots of nooks and crannies so I envisaged some profitable 'hoovering' when they had been cooking.

Through the kitchen was the bathroom that you had to walk through to get to the back of the boat. There was a bath and shower, toilet and washbasin with a large mirror. There was a door at each end so they could be private.

The bedroom had a double bed with plenty of cupboards and wardrobes that had all been painted with flowers by Mum. The walls below the gunwale were deep red and Mum had bought a new bedspread that matched. It all looked really cosy but when I looked at the bed Dad looked at me and said "No". I think I knew what he meant but I vowed to try it out at some stage.

Behind the bedroom were three steps up into a small back cabin with more painted cupboards and an array of little orange and yellow lights. A pair of doors, similar to the first boat, opened onto an even smaller back garden. I was reluctant to wag my tail for fear of wagging myself into the water.

We cruised for two wonderful years on our new boat.

My early days were a nightmare from which, at one time, I thought I would never awaken. I will never forget those times but they no longer govern me. From the moment when Mum first smiled at me I began my life. I think that she and Dad are really just beginning theirs.

We've met some wonderful people and had great adventures. We're in France now and some of you may have read the little bits I persuaded Dad to include in his first book. I am glad to have had the chance to record things from my point of view – I am part of all this after all.

Over the years I have exorcised some ghosts – I think Mum and Dad have too.

We finally lost Bonny when she was sixteen. She died in France and shared some wonderful times with us. She did put her own slant on things in A Barge at Large and we still miss her. She grounded us by giving us unconditional love and friendship and even though we taught her a few tricks, she taught us far more.

I was sacked from the magazine after a contretemps with the new editor. It was basically a clash of personalities though, having spoken to the magazines two regular readers, neither thought I should have been given the boot. The previous editor, Kevin, was a pleasant, discerning chap who recognised raw talent when he saw it, but still invited me to write a column. The new bloke and I did agree that I was basically rubbish but what bought matters to a head (giving him the excuse to fire me) was during the period when I was writing from Holland in January. He wanted tales of bikini-clad beauties lounging on classic boats in the sunshine drinking Pimms. The problem was that we were in central Holland in the middle of winter. My subject matter was folks wrapped in reindeer skins in temperatures of minus 20. I can be relatively creative but there are limits. But what the previous couple of years writing had done was actively force me to record our experiences. Looking back on notes and photographs, even just weeks later, it's astonishing how much I had forgotten. It's not surprising that I fail to recall things, I'm not the sharpest knife in the box so writing things down is a necessity.

Over our dozen boaty years we've met some great people who are fun, generous and kind, like Michel and Lucy in Nancy who helped us out with a poorly dog. They lent us their car to take Bonny to the vet when we'd known them for barely an hour. We've also come across the odd plonker, like the chap who accosted Jan outside a supermarket in Migennes, France. We've seen stunning places that it's impossible to forget like Namur in Belgium but we've also encountered some messy bits, like sections of the Bourbourg Canal near Dunkirk which is truly industrial and smelly. The good outweighs the bad many, many fold but I'll try and give you a balance of each. Despite the fact that we see wonderful things, it's the people who really make the difference.

It's funny, whenever we've left somewhere having lived in a house, there are only a handful of people with whom we really want to keep in touch. With the boat it's different – there's nobody! No, seriously, we've lived in both Holland and France. In Zwartsluis, Holland and St. Jean de Losne, Burgundy, we've lived within the boating community and there are plenty of people in both places we look forward to seeing again and stay friends with. It's complicated a little because of the nature of boating, which is transitory. We, or others, move on and make new friends in new places. But if (and when) we do go back; I like to think we'll have friends who'll share a glass of wine with us. At the very least we're left with some great memories, and the only reason for that is because we made the decision to try something different twelve years ago.

Canal des Vosges

Back on the Canal des Vosges we travelled from Thaon to Charmes in search of (drinking) water and to recharge the (boat) batteries. It was a miserable day – so bad we had to engage the windscreen smearers. These are real technological marvels. Three blades, each a foot long, are driven by three separate 12-volt motors. Each ancient 'power-unit' whines and strains at a different pitch – it's a tortured racket that renders conversation impossible. So idiosyncratic are they, that when I demonstrated them to a friend recently, he nearly collapsed with mirth. When you turn them off, the blades don't return to point zero like those on your car but stop exactly where they are. Hence one may be 'at rest' off to the side (where it's supposed to be) while the others grind to a halt at various points across the scratched, smeared glass – usually conveniently right in your eye line. This is not ideal when approaching a lock in a downpour and crosswind.

What are we doing cruising in foul weather? You might well ask!

Since we left St. Jean, some 200 kilometres ago, we haven't seen a single commercial boat. Just as we moor up at Thaon des Vosges three creep by one after the other. The last one is one of a trio that ply a regular trade along this stretch of canal. They are built-for-purpose bulk carriers that run a 6 kilometre stretch all day from 7.00 am till 7.00pm. Back and forth they go - down empty, back full. They are loaded and unloaded at each end by cranes and appear to be shifting a pile of rocks from one place to the other - but I'm sure there's more to it than that.

While in Thaon I cleaned the boat from top to bottom (or waterline) – 3 hours it took with canal water, brush and rag. On arrival in Charmes a council employee covered the boat in dirty, wet grass while strimming the bank – much to the amusement of some of the 40 camper vans parked next to the canal. They kept on laughing right up to the point where Jan switched on our washing machine and tripped all the electric! There was a team of grass cutters in fact. Strimmer-man, another with a 'walk-behind' and a third on a ride-on mower. Why is it that the fattest one always drives the ride-on? There was real panic as both campers and boaters dashed about moving power lines and ropes to avoid them being mulched.

   A mature, thin Belgian lady arrived last evening with her husband in a sort of caravan. It actually looked like a windowless, white box towed by a small white van. There is a door and a satellite dish on top so it's obviously a 'live-aboard', but on first glance it looks like a dormant burger-van. Dressed in black leather trousers the lady went for a brief bike ride. There was more meat on the cycle frame than her and she looked like a big black letter 'k' astride her silver steed. This morning she's wandering around in her pyjamas. He's a big lad, looks like he could handle himself, so I decide not to go and ask him for a burger.

   We only amble along at 6 or 7 kilometres an hour and love the wildlife. This morning a buzzard came from behind and swooped down right beside the boat to pluck something from the water before flopping off into the trees. A short while later we moored on a small quay in the middle of nowhere in front of a newly renovated house. There was nothing else for miles around except forest. The towpaths are good dog-walking territory as there's normally no sideways escape. You've got the canal on one side and often a stream or fence on the other. Today there was a high fence separating the path from the forest with 'Danger' signs posted periodically. You couldn't see far into the trees and it was a bit spooky. Was the fence to keep in wild boar or deer? Or was it some sort of military training ground? No, it's a paint-balling centre! I suppose if you want to get into ball-painting, the privacy of an isolated forest is as good as anywhere.

   The reason that I was a bit nervous was that while visiting friends near Toulouse a few years ago we'd gone for a walk and came across a patch of forest which was heavily fenced in. There was an open fronted, wooden hut just inside the fence. The ground between the trees was absolutely devastated, chewed up as if a rotavator had been through. There was no ground cover whatsoever. It transpires that the folk who manage the forests fence off sections and introduce wild boar. The boar dig up and eat anything that's not a big tree thereby giving the forest floor chance to regenerate. These creatures are powerful and can be aggressive. They also average over 200 lbs (around 14 stone or 100 kg) – although they can get much bigger. Not around here, but examples have been recorded in Russia and China up to 750 lbs! Couple this with being able to run up to 40 kph, they are not to be trifled with. Periodically the boar need to be rounded up to be moved on to the next patch of fenced forest. The open side of the wooden hut we saw was facing away from the fence so the foresters use a mirror on a pole to look inside to see if the boars are in a threatening mood before they approach. A method of forest management it may be effective, but certainly not for the faint-hearted.

We begin a stretch of 45 uphill locks, each one about 3 metres deep, climbing up through some stunning scenery – if you like fields and forests that is. Because we're all so used to the immediacy of telephone and internet connection, being without both for nearly a week is a bit peculiar. Instead, we have peace and solitude – detached from the real world. Often the only sounds you hear are the twitter of the birds or rustles in the forest. The odd fish slaps the water and the only people you see accompany the occasional boat (2 per day) or cyclists on the superbly surfaced towpath on the opposite side of the canal. The odd VNF van scoots by but usually it's just the three of us with a BBQ and a book. (VNF is the Vois Navigables Francais – the organisation the runs and maintains the French waterways – very well too). My latest tome, read while sitting in the shade of the trees in my chaise-short (don't need a long one), is 'How to annihilate a pork chop'. There are two moorings on this stretch that are particularly lovely. Lay-bys in effect cut back towards the forest where we can get some protection from the forty-degree temperatures. Having time to appreciate the wildlife is one of the joys of a cruise. Tache, our terrier / poodle, has realized that if he runs off he doesn't get fed, so usually stays close by. He still charges after cats and will stop periodically to dig a big hole in search of a rat or mouse, but he's learning. I had to intervene when he came across a snake. It was probably a grass snake, but just in case, I dragged him away.

It's quite tiring as the locks come thick and fast and we have to concentrate but eventually we reach the canal summit and start downhill towards the port of Épinal – which is closed when we finally reach it due to lack of water. Ironically it's chucking it down again.

Boules (pétanque) is archetypal French. In Thaon there is an enormous purpose-built, boules park, 300 metres by 40, set in the shade of mature trees. Within the park there is a magnificent, open-sided wooden structure (50 x 20 metres), floodlit, that allows players to play during inclement weather or into the evening. According to the chap preparing a griddle for his burgers, because today is Monday, it's 'Grand Prix' day. Up to 150 players, ranging from late teenagers to seniors, play in groups of six or eight. They all take it pretty seriously, the only smiles or laughs seem to be of ridicule when a throw goes awry. There are gentle thumps as the steel boules land on the soft shale and staccato 'clacks' echo under the trees as target-men launch attacks in an attempt to scatter carefully placed groupings. Today they play in Thaon, tomorrow another venue and so on through the week. It's a great way to make and preserve friendships - even if, today at least, the burgers got a bit soggy in a late-afternoon cloudburst.

I cycled the 9 kilometres from Thaon back to Épinal. We had visited five years ago when the port was full – busy and bustling. Access is via a 3 km branch which, at present, is shut due to the low water level. Incongruous really as water is pouring over upper lock gates further down the canal indicating a surfeit of water. The port today is virtually deserted, housing just a few long-term residential boats. The lack of visitors is a substantial loss of income for the port – twenty boats at 10 euros per night builds up over the weeks. The port-side cafe and nearby shops must be suffering too.

We meet quite a few Antipodeans who come over to Europe for a year or two. We encountered a lone Australian, Oliver, on his small cruiser. A chatty fellow who told us of a couple of 'moments' he has had en route. The first was when he temporarily tied his boat to a ladder when deep in a lock in order to climb out and affix his locking lines. When he got up the ladder he dropped his rope and at the same instant the boat became detached from the ladder leaving it floating around down in the lock. Fortunately, the boat drifted toward another ladder so he was able to scramble down and re-acquaint himself with his craft. On the other occasion he was helping the lockkeeper open the gates. He was pushing on an extension to the balance beam (the strong arm on a lock gate on which you push to open and close the gate) when it broke off and he tumbled 3 metres down into the lock – luckily into the water and not on top of his boat. 'No problem', he said in his jaunty Antipodean accent, 'I'm a strong swimmer'.

Now in Charmes we had a lovely evening in the company of Linda and Jan (pronounced yan – he's Swedish, she English). They are not boaters but camper-vanners. They live in the very north of Sweden and it's a 14-hour drive to their southern border where they get the ferry across to northern Germany. She is a really gifted musician and soon had my keyboard lit up like the flight-deck on a Jumbo jet. It made sounds I was totally unaware of – actually using the instrument to its capacity for the first time since I've owned it. She also brought along her accordion and played folk and Irish songs for us to sing along to. They are a mirror of other friends, this time she Swedish and he English. Dave is also a very gifted musician playing guitar, keyboard and accordion. Fun nights these music nights – particularly when I don't join in!

Just arrived in Toul where we had an unpleasant incident with an American man. I need to calm down before I write about it.

Right, I'm calm.

We're going up the first of 3 locks into Toul. As you approach a lock there is a 'perch' (basically a chord that hangs over the water on a hangman's frame) that must be twisted to set a lock in operation. We twisted it and began to approach the lock. For some reason however it hadn't registered and the lights remained on red, so we had to reverse and try again. We approached the lock for a second time but once again it didn't register. I was now getting a bit frustrated. There is an emergency telephone up by the lock and we'd just tied up to go and phone for assistance when the green light came on indicating that the lock would now operate. A small barge had come up behind us and followed us into the lock. It's a reasonably deep lock and the chap from the other boat clambered up a ladder and took our ropes. There was him, a lady who was presumably his wife and two guests.

When ascending a lock, you need to make sure you are securely and safely roped up because when water floods in through sluices in the front gate (and sometimes through 'ground paddles' from below), the currents can be fierce and unpredictable. Sometimes the water pushes you back, sometimes the underlying currents surge you forward. You have to rope up properly to prevent you being sloshed around by the currents – particularly when you are sharing the lock with another boat. The lock-side bollards were not ideally spaced for us on this occasion – they do vary from lock to lock. Our fore rope was fine, that one would prevent us being washed back towards the other boat. But we had a problem with the back one, the one that would stop us going too far forward, potentially into the front gates.

I had secured us temporarily via a long rope to our centre bollard and was looking for a safer way to tie up when our companion set the lock in motion. Basically, the longer the rope, the more play there is in it so the less secure you are. I'd told him I wasn't happy but he'd set it going anyway. The currents in this lock pushed us forward quite violently. Forty tonnes of boat need to be secure as moving water is a powerful medium. The line stopping our boat being swashed into the front gates was too long and I had little control. The tension on the line was incredible – it actually left scorch marks on the rope where it had rubbed around our centre bollard. Because we were not properly secured we lurched and crunched around in the lock. Our 'friend' just laughed, basically showing off to his guests. I was a bit wound up and called him something unpleasant. I told him in no uncertain terms that because he had put us in danger we would be doing the next lock on our own.

So, off we went, got in, and tied up. We pulled the bar to set the lock going but our friend had come right in behind us. He was half in half out of the lock, so sensors on the gates prevented them from closing. After a lengthy 'stand-off' we untied and moved forward to reluctantly allow him in behind us. As he was coming in the gates shut on him, trapping their boat amidships. He couldn't move and he had no way off the boat so, a bit churlishly I admit, I left him there to stew for a while before I climbed the ladder and called the emergency number on the nearby lock cabin. It must have been unnerving for his guests to be stuck like that but he was an aggressive bully who got exactly what he deserved. He can put himself in danger all he likes, but when his behaviour threatens Jan and our boat, I get a bit ratty.

However, as they tend to, things quickly improved. It was here in Toul that we met up with old mate Bill Telfer and so had a great couple of days with him. The first night he said, 'come on, there's a big firework display, let's go and watch, I'll show you the best vantage point.' We walked about three kilometres right across town and stood on a bridge. We were 'some distance' from the fireworks and the view was basically obscured by a line of huge plane trees. Apart from the odd refracted glow among the leaves, we could only see the very highest-shot fireworks. I'm absolutely convinced that we'd have been closer if we'd stayed on the boat! And it rained. Luckily Bill is a great guy, one of those with a laugh that makes you join in, so we did, tittering away on his back deck with a glass of something unpleasant and a lump of cheese.

Loto!

Different places have different ways of doing things. Even the simplest tasks – like buying a drink for example. In the UK you go to the bar, order and pay on the spot. This presumably is in case you dash outside with your pint, jump in the car and bugger off. There's not a great deal of trust placed in the customer. Different on the continent where they stack receipts under an ashtray, tot it up at the end and you pay in one go.

Local people are often rather suspicious of incomers. It's not surprising really, especially in my case. A scrubbily dressed, portly chap with spiky hair would alarm those with the strongest constitutions. What I try and do is offer something first – a smile or a friendly word can open the door. But even that is different from country to country. In Zwartsluis, Holland, where we lived for a couple of years, when you encounter a stranger on the street they will look you in the eye. It's almost a surly stare. No smile, nothing said, just a stare. This is their greeting. It took me 18 months to understand that they weren't being ignorant, just Dutch! Making eye contact is their way of saying hello. If you do get to know them of course you smile and exchange a word or two. It didn't help that I barely spoke a word of their language so relied on their being able to speak mine. I knew a few words but greeting someone with '1,2,3 bread, thank you' would probably have made things worse. At least I speak a little French and I can bluff my way through a basic conversation using the language of a 5-year-old child.

We have noticed that schoolchildren in both countries are unfailingly polite, which is great to see.

LOTO!

One of our great joys is joining in. We do try and mix, getting involved not just with 'expat games', but local events too. One that actually combined the two was when a bunch of us went to The Loto in St. Jean de Losne. This was an eye-opener.........

Tingling with anticipation we arrived at the Salle Polyvalente (community centre that you find in virtually all French towns) for an evening of 'Loto' – which is basically Bingo.

Why?......... You might well ask.

Well, money was being raised for 'Lions International', a fabulous organisation that helps and funds projects both locally and internationally. Caroline, one of our number, who used to boat but now lives in a house nearby, is a 'facilitator' for the Lions and we were supporting her.

In St. Jean de Losne the Lions fund a local telephone helpline. It is a service, manned by volunteers, which supports both the expat community and visitors in times of trouble. Not if your engine needs a new alternator, rather for people with psychological or personal difficulties. For example, when a partner dies or becomes ill, a foreign land can be a confusing and frightening place and this phone line is a place to seek help. It's a great service and the volunteers lend a confidential and compassionate ear – for some people in our community it has literally been a lifeline.

So that's why - now how? What is French Loto? This is more difficult.

The entrance hall looks a bit like the reception area of a 'mostly abandoned' hospital - but cleaner. We were faced initially with a substantial heap of blue 'Bingo' cards on a large table. It was obvious what they were but not how they integrated into the French Loto format. There were a dozen or so of us expats discussing said format with the 'Three Wise Men' on the registration trestle.

Right! Now concentrate. All in Euros - you could buy one Loto card for 6, two for 11, three for 16 and so on. In addition, there were much bigger cards that incorporated 6 cards on a single card – and these were yellow – and cost 25 (or was it 30?). If you bought a big yellow one you got a blue one free. Then there were 'Bingo' cards (as opposed to Loto cards). These were much smaller like a folding 'calling' card, also yellow, incorporating a miniature Loto card and a secret tear-off strip that revealed 3 hidden numbers. I'm not sure any of us actually figured out what these were for – except as a way of raising an extra few Euros for the Lions. The wise men explained, both in words of too many syllables and too quickly, how things were done.

We weren't much the wiser when we shuffled towards the main arena - having parted with an average of 20 Euros per couple for a 'mystery tour' of foreign Loto.

There are situations where a minimal command of the language is helpful. Some of us struggle with our native tongue so these increasingly bewildering exchanges were 'difficult' and the Tower of Bable slowly crumbled. Our payment receipt and various-coloured cards were stamped by another official seated at another trestle table at the entrance to the main hall. Finally, we were officially registered as official players. Exhausted, we repaired to a table to recuperate. We'd got the timing a bit wrong and had arrived an hour early. At least it gave us the chance to limber up and do some gentle stretching exercises.

There was a 'snack-bar' in the corner offering goodies that your cardiovascular specialist would have frowned at. Filled baguettes, French fries, crepes and other delicacies including bottled beer and beverages (not that anyone of sane mind drinks tea here). We (all English save for a lone Antipodean) had been advised to bring along our own snacks and drinks. Consequently, our table soon looked like the buffet at a down-market wedding – a right old mishmash ranging from paté sandwiches to Maltesers and a variety of liquid refreshment. For example, I brought along my wine in an old Grolsch bottle, one of those with a clip-over top. It was from a box, purchased at little expense from a local garden centre – a wine of uncertain parentage that would be most unwelcome in any fine establishment.

In total there was seating for perhaps 200 people at 18 long tables and they were mostly full. We foreigners nibbled and imbibed and, a little unsure of how things were to proceed, looked like an outing from an establishment for the bewildered.

Nearly an hour later excitement reached fever pitch as the PA system spluttered into life. It sounded like the lady announcer was sitting underwater inside a garden shed some distance away and, notwithstanding the language difficulties, it was almost impossible to understand the rules. Perhaps if you're brought up with it there's no problem, but it appeared that the regulations had been mauled by three or four layers of French bureaucracy before arriving at our table. At one point most eyes in the room turned to us so I can only presume that the lady announcer had just warned the natives to steer clear of our table.

So, apprehensive but refreshed, off we went. The Lady Announcer sat behind an air-blown storm of balls in a glass case, atop a raised bench – she looked like a Judge with her half-moon glasses and fierce hairdo. She was accompanied by her Loto Recorder who ensured fair play. Before beginning in earnest, she called out a series of letters. If these corresponded to one printed on the reverse of any of your cards, you were awarded another card – just to add to the blizzard of papers.

Then our problems really began - she called out the first number. Three or four of us had rudimentary French so it was our duty to help out the less fluent. Down our end of the table (I sat on the end suspecting that, at some stage, I would have to dash out and calm down), I whispered the numbers to my wife next door, who in turn passed on the information to her neighbours, both of whom are a bit hard of hearing. Having deaf people in the middle of a whispering snake was a bad idea. Most of the information got through unscathed but it was a bit of a Chinese whispers situation and at times there was some confusion. It really became shambolic when my wife 'pre-guessed' the translation incorrectly so the wrong number was passed on. This meant a hastily-whispered correction, by which time the next number had been called, and the whole house of cards gradually collapsed. Thus, our carefully designed system disintegrated and we'd have to wait for the next game.

You keep the same cards for the duration of the evening and rather than crossing the numbers off with a pen you cover each correctly called number with transparent tiddlywinks (which we also had to purchase!). The tiddlywinks are light so you have to be careful not to sneeze or you carefully crafted game-card could become a shambles. One lady nudged her big yellow card with her bosom shunting the tiddlywinks onto the wrong numbers so she had to abandon that game. Another (male this time) lost track of the translations (and mistranslations) and got in such a muddle he swept all his tiddlywinks off his card and sat in a huff with his arms folded across his chest for the remainder of that game.

Each 'game' had three segments. Firstly, competitors try to complete one line on any of their cards. If someone 'gets a line up' the numbers are checked by a man with a roving microphone. He comes and stands by the table and calls out the numbers to the recorder lady who verifies them up on her bench in the distance. If the numbers are correct the winner is awarded a pork chop. In the second segment two lines must be completed and in the third, all three (for a full house). Numbers are checked after each segment by roving-mic-man and various pieces of meat are awarded. The size of animal lump increased with each segment so a Full House winner could expect at least a haunch. We had a collective insecure moment regarding what to shout out if one of us completed a segment. 'House', or 'Housey Housey' is shouted in the UK – but yelling 'Maison' would have been plain ridiculous – and we'd probably have been drummed out for taking the mickey. No, what you actually shout is 'Oui' (yes). Not that it bothered any of us - I was rather suspicious that certain strategic numbers had been omitted from our cards. None of us won a single thing all evening and we probably had thirty or forty cards between us.

Actually, that's not fair - we would have won twice had it not been for a couple of administrative cock-ups. On the first occasion one of our contingent (male but nameless) had two lines up - but thought he was going for a full house. Consequently, he failed to yell 'Oui!' - and missed out on a black pudding. Secondly a lady (who was completing a card for someone else because the true owner was overwhelmed) got a full house. Unfortunately, while passing the card back to her friend – thereby allowing the card owner to grab the glory when she yelled out 'Oui!', all the tiddlywinks came off and she was given a bemused shake of the head by roving-mic-man when he came to check the numbers that were now in completely the wrong place. Needless to say, we were all in a fit of giggles. Thereafter the fight seemed to go out of us as concentration waned and our final opportunity had gone.

To be fair, I'm being a bit disparaging about the prizes. It wasn't all hunks of meat. There were food processors, vacuum cleaners, vouchers for local shops etc. etc. - so in fact it was worth concentrating. There were some 'professional' players there who travel from town to town playing various Lotos and win regularly, selling on their prizes on Ebay or Le bon Coin (literally the good corner), a French alternative. It's possibly not surprising that we amateurs wandered home empty-handed.

The first 'Game' (3 segments – one line, two lines, full house) took about 12 minutes – and it turned out there were 18 games! The snack-bar had run dry and some of us were near comatose by the time midnight arrived and we were released. Two of us needed to call the emergency telephone number for guidance but overall, another four hours of a long winter had passed in confusion and harmony.

In the final analysis we have helped the Lions and, despite being poorer and prizeless, we can hold up our heads with pride. (Pride see! A little gentle wordplay to augment the tale.)

The dog had trashed the wheelhouse when we got home. At this stage he was still rather new to being left alone. We have a multi-fuel fire so I have adapted the gates, built for our wheelhouse doors, to fit across the entrance to the lounge from the kitchen. We couldn't risk him throwing toys or blankets around where there is a hot fire blazing. Tache was therefore confined to the kitchen and wheelhouse while we were out – I admit that we hadn't expected the Loto evening to last four hours, but that notwithstanding, the dear old dog had obviously had 'separation issues'. Stacked in the wheelhouse were two garden sacks full of logs for the fire. These had been 'dismantled' so walking into the wheelhouse and kitchen was like clambering over a huge log flume, the like of which you see on Canadian rivers. Although I did, it's not really fair to blame the dog. Nowadays when we go out without him, we lock him in his cage with Dennis, his smiling toy donkey.

St. Jean Reflections

I feel I must reflect a little on our time in St. Jean de Losne. Most people who have either boated or researched inland boating will probably have heard of St. Jean. As with many walks of life, dissenting voices are the loudest and I do hear grumbles about this and that but others, like me, who love the place normally just enjoy it and keep quiet. Yes, most people seem to like the place – in our case we enjoyed five wonderful years in the company of some great people.

Boaters come from all walks of life – a wide range of professions, nationality and background. Everyone has a story to tell and it's usually far more interesting to listen than talk. Everyone is here because a love of boating so if worldly conversation dries up we can talk about boating problems – usually culminating with lavatories. We visit other boats or people come to us. We gather at social functions or just pass while strolling or walking the dog.

In St Jean there is a medium through which inmates keep in touch with one another. By medium I don't mean Mystic Maureen beaming spiritual enlightenment through the ether. No, I'm referring to Radio Gare d'Eau.

At 9.30 every morning anticipation reaches fever pitch as people switch on their VHF radios and wait for a familiar refrain to drift over the locale....

"Is this channel in use?"

It can be a bit quiet around St. Jean at times, particularly during winter months, so it's nice to know we are not alone.

Volunteer announcers take on the onerous task of anchoring this communication super-highway. It is public-service broadcasting of 'crucial importance' to the boating community and available to anyone with a radio

– all they have to do is tune to channel 77 and be awake at 9.30 am – a task beyond some I do admit.

Firstly, the announcer asks if people will 'check into the net' on a boat-by-boat basis. Those who respond say good morning, state their name and boat name. This is important because it reassures everyone that the crew of that particular boat is still alive. With temperatures of minus double-digits during the night, we rely heavily on heating appliances to keep going and any malfunction could be life-threatening. I have to say that I'm not actually aware of anyone freezing to death and there's not much anyone could do if someone had, but it's reassuring to hear familiar voices.

It is difficult to determine the state of some boaters' well-being because 9.30 appears an hour or two early for some residents. Some sound as if their radio check-in is being conducted from within a duvet, others like they've contracted an unpleasant throat disease. But a croak is better than silence.

So, once we've established that everyone is alive and there are no emergencies, we move on to the pith of the broadcast. Promoting social events for example. There is usually something going on, from meeting up at the book-swap twice a week or Tai chi or art classes.

The 'Pudding Club' is a relatively new one. A volunteer organiser picks a theme – Easter or winter for example – then determines what kind of creation should reflect that theme – a cake or a pie perhaps. Offerings are delivered to the book-swap, above the museum on the High Street, on Wednesday morning for judging. Major cash prizes are available for the winning entry and though the amount doesn't even cover the cost of ingredients, it's nice to win something.

Judging is very subjective of course. You can make the most magnificent fish pie only to discover that one of the judges is allergic to fish, or a vegan. There are many very good cooks amongst our number but it's really the taste that matters. A tasty pie looking like someone's trodden in it will beat a bland item that looks like an art-deco masterpiece every time. Everyone present, whether competitors or not, wants to taste everything, so by lunchtime everyone is stuffed to the gills (particularly if it's fish pie).

One guy, who shall remain nameless, is a very accomplished cook. Sadly, he has yet to win a competition despite submitting a number of entries – he even chose his own judges one week! One time he had taken ages to make a delicious pie which he'd hand-crafted with love and care and was very tasty - only to be beaten by my wife who had knocked something up in ten minutes the previous afternoon using tinned pears and various random items found lurking in a cupboard. Sometimes there is no justice.

I did join in once. Normally I manage to make a perfectly respectable set of ingredients look like a compost heap but on this occasion I followed a TV chef's recipe for chicken pie to the letter - but came second. I subsequently wrote to him saying that if he couldn't even beat my wife, what the hell was he doing on television. I received no apology. Despite disappointments such as this, these occasions are just another way to cement friendships and pass a fun couple of hours. Gastroenteritis can be a thorn in the side, buy hey, we're tough cookies.

A couple of times a year the Gare d'Eau plays host to a sizeable event. (Gare D'eau translates as water station. It is basically a large, off-river basin that used to be a haven and loading area for commercial boats. These days it is home to around 250 private moorers and a boat-hire base). One such event may be an 'open day' (or Portes Ouverts in French – literally open doors) where local boat-related businesses showcase their wares or have a sales drive for boats on brokerage. Various stalls appear round the port selling wicker baskets, regional wine, jam and the like. In addition, the 'bric-a-brac' crowd arrives – these are the equivalent of car-boot or garage sales. You can find all sorts of useless stuff here and the quality of goods on offer is rarely in doubt – basically down the budget end. They often look like a 'Closing Down Sale' from a rubbish dump. But if you want a spigot from a 1940's dishwasher or an old saw with no teeth, here's where you'll find them.

River Rats is the local group, mainly boaters, who meet once a month (except during high summer when most people are away cruising) to plan social activities such as quiz nights or the occasional treasure hunt. The 'committee' of five or six stalwarts (some willing) is democratically elected by the oligarch, a wonderful lady in her tenth decade.

There is generally one stall ('general household goods', for want of a less accurate description) whose proceeds go to River Rats. This is when a call goes out over Radio Gare d'Eau for volunteers to both man the stall and provide goods for sale. It's at this point that the airwaves go a bit quiet, as if the call to arms has blown a collective fuse. In fact, the only people who respond are those with a genuine excuse not to get involved.

The community thrives on its social scene which provides fun distractions. Sometimes people are a bit reluctant to suggest a new ideas because they will invariably be lumbered with organising the damn thing. Like my mates Paul and Mal who suggested a treasure hunt. 'Great, get on with it then,' was the enthusiastic response! And hey presto, a month later we have a hoard of (mainly) English-registered cars parked in farmyards or fields having got completely lost.

Radio Gare d'Eau was started (I believe) by a guy called Mike Hoffman who had been involved with a similar set-up in Beaucaire, a port down the southern end of the River Rhone, not far south of Avignon. Sadly, Mike passed away recently but the real raison d'être of the community was highlighted when people rallied round and helped him, both practically and morally, when he became frail. He was a fascinating man with a wealth of experience and knowledge on many matters, not least boats and navigation – and he'll be sadly missed.

Actually, the core members of River Rats are not boaters at all. They are local residents who give their energy for free and without whom the whole thing would probably collapse. But I guess for them, being expats, it's a great way to make friends with boaters who come and go for days, weeks, even years. People don't need help when things are ticking over, it's when things go wrong in an unfamiliar land that we need back up. In fact, it's only when we need help that some of us realize these folks are there at all. I'm sure many of the things they've done have gone unnoticed but it's thanks to them that we, as transient boaters, can live our care-free existence. I'm not going to single anyone out; you know who you are. Should any of you read this, thank you.

I'm fortunate enough to speak some rudimentary French and have offered my services to one or two people. It's good to help, you feel part of things.

It doesn't all go well though like when my mate Ken bought a car of suspect parentage. He took me along as translator to the local garage three times and each visit cost 300 Euros (oil pump, alternator and tyres) – more than the car was worth! I wasn't invited a fourth time. Actually, I was, but he couldn't get the car started.

Lovely guy Ken. He and his wife Rhonda invited me and others onto their boat for my 50th birthday bash. Ken died recently – RIP mate.

One thing we're asked is, what do we do with ourselves all the time? Well, apart from day to day living which includes chopping and collecting wood for the fire, general boat maintenance and managing to fit in the odd social function, there are many things of interest locally. Like Ken, we have a knackered old motor car and we regularly clatter around Burgundy (and further afield) in search of enlightenment.

Dijon is half an hour away by train or car. What a great city that is. There's mustard of course which nicely complements the annual gastronomic fare where you can sample delights such as horse or snails – foods of vastly differing velocity – and appeal! Dijon was home to Gustave Eiffel who built many railway bridges, and a certain tower of course. He also designed the magnificent covered market (Les Halles) in the city centre. The city has some lovely architecture and is well known for its 'Toits Bourguignons' which are roofs made from glazed, multi-coloured tiles (often green, yellow and black) arranged in geometric patterns. You see the like throughout Burgundy. It's an ancient, lovely city kept fresh by its university students. There's also an Ikea where you can have hours of misery getting lost and battling meatballs.

Beaune is another lovely town, known as the wine capital of Burgundy. About half an hour from St. Jean, it's a walled town and famous for its architecturally acclaimed hospice, which is now a museum. We visited the town last spring. We left St. Jean on a balmy spring morning, Jan, her daughter Carly and me. Being a 'touristy' trip, we were full of the joys and wearing shorts. Beaune is higher than St. Jean and the temperature nearer freezing than was comfortable for our chosen attire. We all had goose bumps like duck eggs as we soldiered on - straight to an indoor cafe for a restorative. We did stand out a bit as the locals, almost without exception, were muffled up in varieties of dead animal skins.

Carly had flown into Geneva, about 2-hours by car from St. Jean. If you go the mountain route you are treated to one of the finest views in Europe (to me anyway). As you top the Jura mountains and begin to descend toward Geneva, the city and lake are spread before you in an amazing panorama. The Swiss Alps stand mighty and crystalline in the background and aeroplanes coming into the airport look like tiny insects as they cross the lake far, far below. The road, particularly on the Swiss side is rather twisty and steep so you need to choose the day to go as the weather up there can be rather changeable (to be polite).

There is a hotel part way down the Swiss side on whose terrace you can 'take tea' and take in the fabulous vista – when it's not snowing of course.

By going the Jura route to Geneva airport, you can avoid paying for a vignette (motorway license) in Switzerland by sneaking in the 'side door' of the airport. If you arrive by auto-route from France you have to pay about £35 for a 12-month license just to travel about 2 kilometres of Swiss motorway! If you've sneaked in but return via the motorway route you don't need a license to get out of Switzerland. The motorway drive is almost as spectacular with lengthy tunnels and wonderful mountain views as you head back towards Bourg-en-Bresse in eastern France.

Where did you start?

Another thing that people ask me is how we went about buying our barge – well, here you go.....

Rough Guide to Buying a Barge

We had three fabulous years on our narrowboats, so good in fact that we said goodbye and sold up. Our UK narrowboat adventures are documented in A Narrowboat at Large. I started writing at the 'pre-totally-knackered-middle-age stage' - before reaching the 'totally-incompetent-late-middle-age-stage'. Same with the boats really, we want to get on with things and enjoy it before we get too creaky and the money runs out. So, we decided to buy a barge and argue with people in different countries.

Now please be warned, this is strictly a 'novice barge-buyers rough guide' (although if you want to start from a complete shell and do all the work yourself, it may equally be a 'novice's guide to owning a rough barge'). It is a personal warts and all account of how we did it - follow at your peril. So, here goes....

We started with Google, because that required no physical effort, where a bewildering variety of vessel was revealed. Roughly €20,000 will buy you the 'challenge' of a rotting steel leviathan the size of a supermarket into which you can empty your bank account. Quadruple that figure, add a zero and you can buy the ultimate in barging luxury. At the very top end you really are in the stratosphere. In fact, I subsequently came across a 30-metre yacht (not a barge admittedly) that was costing the new owner 30 million Euros – yes, that's one million Euros per metre!). The only thing you can do is work out your budget, stick to it, and let the Scandinavian supermarket owners get on with it. You can have lots of fun with a couple of old oil drums and a plank of wood but there is plenty in between.

Types of barge include Aak, Klipper, Steilsteven, Luxe Motor, Beurtschip, Katwijker, Westlander, Tjalk and Hagenaar, Humber, Thames and more. Blimey!

What we needed were some parameters and after taking advice we joined the DBA (Dutch Barge Association which is a non-profit organisation for anyone interested in barging). The DBA, for us, has been invaluable and their Barge Buyers Handbook enabled us to flesh out our skeletal knowledge. (When not being used for reference it was popped under the leg of our coffee table to arrest an annoying wobble. As with many things I've built there is often an annoying wobble).

Roughly, we narrowed our requirements down to this: a motorboat (as opposed to sail) with a wheelhouse, big enough to live on (but not too costly to run) and capable of travelling most of the waterways of continental Europe. We set our maximum dimensions at 20m x 4.20m x 1m x 2.7m (length, width, draft and air-draft). The engine had to be strong enough to cope with the larger rivers and we wanted a bow-thruster. The electrical, gas and plumbing specifications should be good - or the price low enough for us to upgrade within budget. AND we want to cruise this season.

We can't afford a newly built barge, nor a recently built second hand one, due to budgetary constraints so it appears we're limited to an original ex-working barge. Let's say for arguments sake that our 'finished' budget is £80,000 (100,000 Euros based on a compromise exchange rate). Based on initial searches, these old boats vary enormously even within our parameters. Older working barges, some of which date back to the 1860's, were built of iron. The1920's (and the advent of the Luxe-Motor) saw barges built mainly from steel. Sadly, for us modern buyers, starting around fifty years ago, many of the originals were scrapped when the Dutch Government decided to 're-align' the barge trade. At the same time, it also offered compensation to the owners of small barges still carrying to convert them from working barges to something else, often houseboats. This is why there are not that many unconverted small barges around. Although many originals have undoubted charm and character, anything up to a hundred years old might well have 'condition and on-going maintenance issues' (to be generous). Indeed, one persons 'historic charm' might be another person's 'knackered'.

So, concentrating on matching our self-imposed criteria rather than shape at this stage, we looked afresh and full of excitement, we found our first 'target' in the sun-kissed resort of Rickmansworth. To be frank it was a disappointment (the boat, not Rickmansworth). It was a mess because it was moored under a sappy tree, it was also too narrow and too expensive for us to upgrade. Nice shape though – a Steilsteven.

As a back-up we'd arranged to meet a chap on a yellow bridge in Docklands who was to show us round some barges and impart wisdom. I've never been good at retaining information, preferring to swan through life unburdened by the weight of knowledge, so I was glad my mate Alan was there (I'd invited him as my voice of reason and memory bank) and between us we managed to pick up a few things. We were dressed like narrowboaters and looked like Hill Billy and Hill Benny as we shuffled among the clickety-clackety heels and smart suits of the banking fraternity at Canary wharf. They lunch on the likes of 'green-lipped warthog and Ionian watercress wraps' from the outrageously priced deli's, while we had ham butties and a can of John Smiths Bitter supplied by my wife. We ate while sitting on the wall of a grubby fountain and watched the beautiful people glide by.

The guy we were meeting imports barges from Holland and shows us some impressive specimens clearly in the 'out of our price' bracket. We were shown inside one, a part-finished conversion project the size of an aircraft hangar, which to be frank would have taken me about thirty years to complete – too much money, too much time. It is this man that Jan and I are to meet the following week in the Netherlands when he will show us some boats he has sourced via his network of 'skippers'. We are to send him a list of 'roughly what we want' and he'll do the rest.

We're really excited - we were going, by ferry, to look at our first boats on foreign soil, well not soil exactly ....

We saw four, the first of which was enormous (at nearly 50 metres) but it was the interior that took our breath away. It looked as if it had either been a movie set or inhabited with someone with a psychological irregularity. The main cabin contained a huge iron fire-canopy, suspended from the deck above on thick chains, which formed the centrepiece of a sort of indoor, open fire. Large, rounded rocks were placed in the approximate shape of the 'devil's fireplace' and it looked like something the druids would frolic around, drinking and shagging. The remaining interior was crafted from randomly plonked railway sleepers masquerading as seats, tables and a sort of work-bench thing! Oh, and a cabin at the blunt end with about 18 inches of headroom. Lucky to avoid a nasty splinter, the skipper sat on a sleeper and looked thoughtfully at the huge fireplace. I had specified that our limit was 20 metres so I questioned why we were viewing this monster. 'Well, you never know,' he replied.

The other three we saw were variously, a sailing tjalk (which, if a sailing tjalk was what we were after, we both agreed that we couldn't have seen a finer example), a lined shell (no insulation) that needed an engine and complete re-fit – and would have ended up way over budget - and lastly a monstrous hulk that that I had no idea where to start with. To be honest, we'd been asked to provide a brief and what we'd been shown didn't really measure up so it was a bit disappointing. The only reason this trip was useful was so we wouldn't book another trip with this chap.

Our next sortie would last five days and would be the 'biggie' - time to convert the countless hours of internet work and ingested knowledge into reality. Planned with military precision, the trip got off to an indifferent start when the budget flight was delayed by an hour (and ours was the first of the day!). Then it couldn't land because it was too windy and the pilot intercommed, 'Sorry, the wind is over safe limits, we'll have to go round again'. We were only a few feet from the runway as the engines whined to get us up again. A neighbouring passenger thoughtfully puked into her paper bag - prompting her mate to follow suit. Suffice to say that when we finally got out of the airport we were tempted to cancel the first viewing and head for a café in Amsterdam to seek solace. Added to this was the fact that, because we had so much paperwork, I'd tried to check in for our flight in Birmingham with our emergency lavatory paper. The BMI Lady asked, 'are you sure that no-one has interfered with your luggage sir?' No, this trip was taking off where the previous one ended – in a bit of a shambles.

But we soldiered on. We had pre-arranged six viewings - not that straightforward considering the limiting criteria we had set ourselves. During this trip we drove 1500 kilometres from Tholen (pronounced tollan) in the south to Delfzijl (pronounced delfs file - roughly) in the far north to Harlingen in the far West and every ship we viewed was a 'nearly'. Much closer to our requirements than our earlier trip, but so far, not quite. Delfzijl, way up in the North-East is, according to one Dutch friend, the place at the edge of the world where you go when you've failed everywhere else. Alarmingly we fitted right in and spent two hours chatting with a chap who was looking at making furniture out of seaweed - no, didn't mean much to us either.

Most people speak English which is a good job because our vocal set-up is not geared to the guttural Dutch language - if you do have a go at the odd word you end up spitting at someone, which even in this open-minded country may cause offence.

While looking, three ship owners were in tears at giving up their pride and joy. One guy was retiring, one lady was very poorly and the other's spouse wanted to buy a motor-home instead. They were all passionate and proud of their vessels.

So, six viewings and only 'possibles' but it was while staying in Franeker (near Harlingen, where the skipper had haggled over the price of the room and won a notable victory) that we found a seventh 'possible' on an obscure Dutch web site. We arranged to view the ship while on our way back to the airport. On the internet we could see the photo (because that was in English) but the Dutch text wasn't much help. Anyhow, we looked and liked and it seemed a good compromise. Sadly, this guy is selling because he has developed rheumatoid arthritis.

She's called Vrouwe Johanna and is a Groninger Boltjalk (hull supposedly shaped a bit like a clog). We're called Jo and Janna so 'Johanna' is close enough. Besides we're both Lancastrians so we can drop the 'h'. It ticked most of our boxes and seems technically OK but needed plenty of work inside to lower it to our previous standards. This is in complete contrast to the author who is technically not very good and needs work on the outside.

The interiors of the boats we viewed varied enormously from the bizarre to the tired to the non-existent. The most impressive main cabin was on the sailing tjalk, hardwood throughout and cosy but that was accompanied by a bedroom that was about four feet high and a bathroom you wouldn't let a rat into. Often the interiors were a bit '1960's', rather like the house in which great aunt Maude has lived happily for forty years unaware that the décor is slipping into a time-warp. Bear in mind we are looking exclusively at boats within our budget, so you really can't expect a palace. Vrouwe Johanna's interior is OK for a holiday boat but as live-aboard it needs a good deal of upgrading, which we'll do gradually. This is the kind of stuff that I can tackle.

Now the fun started. We engaged a surveyor to do an appraisal, both value and technical, which came back positive.

We made an offer at which the vendor 'humphed' and spluttered before we settled on a compromise. Then our problems really begin as we enter the mythical world of a contract, a Memorandum of Agreement, which lays out each party's responsibilities. Had we been buying through a broker, they would have come up with a contract and we would have then engaged a Notary to look over it and handle the legal side of things (like de-registration from the Kadaster, the Dutch ship's register). But this was a 'private sale' so we engaged a broker to act on our behalf and draw up the contract, using their notary for the fiddly bits.

We obviously have to insure the vessel and most companies insist on an in-depth survey performed by a recognised surveyor and especially a minimum 'below-water-line' steel thickness, which we insisted was written into the contract.

When the draft contract arrived by email it looked like someone had pushed the wrong button on the 'translation programme' as it bore scant resemblance to the English I was taught as a boy but after a lengthy bout of email tennis we sorted it out.

Contract agreed and signed, we transferred the total purchase price to the notary who acts as 'financial referee'. He will only release the money to the vendor when our surveyor is happy that the boat is sound and any necessary repair work is done to his, and our, satisfaction - AND after he has de-registered the boat from the Dutch Kadaster and paid off any outstanding loans or mortgage on the ship. Simple!

Right, time for a survey. Tom finds a suitably expensive boatyard and arranges for the vendor to deliver the ship. We can't drive it there because at this stage we are neither insured or qualified – nor indeed the owners. Tom suggests I be there while he surveys so he can talk me through it (which is unusual I believe) so another trip is organised. Costs mounting up - and if the surveyor condemns the thing we're back to square one!

There are a couple of minor problems that will be tacked to the contract as addenda (and signed by both parties) and the faults must be rectified before our money disappears. A little disconcertingly, toward the end of the sea trial, the surveyor is piloting the boat slowly back towards a mooring in a stiff breeze among millions of Euros worth of cruisers, when, because the bow-thruster isn't working because the generator is winterized, we end up drifting sideways down a narrow arm sideways!

The vendor buys me lunch and we talk about him giving up his boat, about us buying it and how if he hadn't liked us, we wouldn't have got this far. Reassuringly he tells me that he will spend all the time I need teaching me about the boats systems. He's a prison officer and a gentleman and there are tears in his eyes - he's sad to be giving up his boat, and I am determined to respect that.

While all the above is going on there are a few other things to look at. Firstly, we have to have a licence to drive the thing. This comes in the form of an ICC (International Certificate of Competence) with CEVNI endorsement (Code Européen des Voies Navigable Intérieure) which is a highway code of the European Waterways. You have to do a practical handling course and pass the written CEVNI test (multiple guess, 11/14 required). In addition, we require a VHF Operators Licence and a Ships Radio Licence. The boat has to be de-registered in Holland and re-registered on the SSR (Small Ships Register) in the UK providing that we have a UK address, are a UK citizen and our ship is under 24m). When all this is done we have to arrange insurance, then get ourselves to Holland and hope we don't steer the thing straight into a gravel barge.

On most of our viewings we were accompanied by professional and friendly brokers. The owners we met privately were proud, pleasant people all too often giving up their boats because they were being forced to do so through age or illness. We approached our travels around the marinas and boatyards of Holland with nervous anticipation but treated our wanderings as part of our great boating adventure.

From what we've seen we really like the country - 25% of it is below sea-level and it is green and very flat. The majority of the population lives in the South-West corner, all in all a bit like a snooker table with a leg missing.

Be warned though, on top of the purchase price of our barge we've had have a number of

unwelcome additions approximately as follows (2007):

Four 'steerage' trips to Holland (3 as a couple and one solo including flights, ferries, car hire, fuel, accommodation and food) £1,400.

Broker and notary £1,100

Survey £870 (including pre-purchase appraisal and boat lift)

ICC and CEVNI qualifications from £120 pp dependent of experience (T.R. Boat Handling – superb)

VHF Operators licence course £180

UK SSR registration (Small Ships Register) £25

Insurance @ £500.

In addition to all this, when you've bought your boat there will be up-grade / alteration costs. There will also be on-going costs such as fuel, mooring, maintenance and navigation charges.

It's fair to say that the process was far more involved than we imagined, everything from research to getting the dog a passport took a great deal of effort - enjoyable in a masochistic kind of way, but really quite complicated and protracted.

Having said all that, we couldn't wait to go back to Holland and get on with it! Just need to find a decent ale.

End of an Era

Back to the present....
 Heading for new territory again. This time the Marne au Rhin Canal which flows east / west between Toul and Vitry-le-François. Initially it's rather like an 'A' road, in other word a means to an end rather than breath-taking - it's also weedy. But where it's weedy the water is incredibly clear and shoals of fish, some a good size, swim in the shallows. It is a problem for our engine water filters which have to emptied regularly. As with many boats, water is pumped from the waterway, round the engine to cool it and then out of the exhaust. If it all gets blocked up it can cause the engine to overheat so you have to stop and clear the filters. You can see the weed hanging and dripping off the lock gates, almost like some exotic eastern water garden (that's eastern as in Japan, not Grimsby) - if it weren't such a nuisance I would appreciate it better. Someone told me that the amount of weed is due to agricultural chemicals, fertilizers and the like, being washed into the canals. I'm not sure about that but, either side of the Mauvages tunnel, which is the summit pound of the canal, the weed is at its worst. Seen from a canal bridge on a sunlit morning you can see that a channel has literally been ploughed through the weed, chopped away by boat's propellers. The canal is perfectly still and the sunlight illuminates an underwater Eden frozen in the water. It's like a swamped forest and you can see fish weaving between the stems.

 The other thing we see in the water is jellyfish – thousands of them. At least to you and me they're jellyfish. They are about 20mm across, transparent with a pliable white 'skeleton' and swim with the pulse of a jellyfish. Craspedacusta sowerbyi they are called officially and though not strictly jellyfish, we had one or two swimming around in our water filter – like having our own private little aquarium.

Still on the nature trail, while moored in Void (where we availed ourselves of VNF's stray Wifi signal) I saw a genuine European Wild Cat while out walking the dog. Not a feral domestic one but a proper mottled, ring-tailed model. Rather larger and stockier than a normal cat they are elusive creatures and I believe and it's rare to see one. It's a good job the dog didn't spot it otherwise there could have been an altercation.

Some stretches of canal are pretty isolated and we were just rising in a lock on such a stretch when a VNF van pulled up. Oh god, I thought, what have we done now? Well, nothing as it turns out. When we'd paid over 500 Euros for a vignette (cruising license) I thought to advertise the fact by purchasing a new VNF pennant to fly from our mast – the previous one had not stood up to a Burgundian winter and was flapping around like a tatty, light blue rag. It seems that these flags are nearly as rare as the European Wild Cat and I'd asked at every VNF depot along the way if they could provide one. Each referred me to an office I'd already visited, or one I was due to visit. I'd cycled miles to try and find a diminutive little flag and had actually given up the search a couple of weeks ago. But, though some things in socialist France often happen at a conservative pace, they do usually happen eventually. In this instance also as the VNF man was delivering a flag for us. With a big smile on his face said, 'Voila monsieur!', and off he went.

It is a large flag, so big in fact so that we can barely see where we're going when it's flapping about in the breeze from a modified broomstick at the front of the boat. What makes this gift slightly ironic however is that we've recently made the decision to quit France and go to Belgium. The decision is 'spur of the moment' really. We've had five great years in St. Jean de Losne and when we set off this year we had every intention of returning. We'll leave some good friends behind but to go back would mean travelling canals we've experienced already and, much as we have enjoyed them, it's time for something new. We know we've made the right decision because the 'nervy tingles' have kicked in at the prospect of new challenges, including some big waterways.

En route I sent out numerous emails to friends saying that we wouldn't be coming back. The replies were less numerous and ranged from (apparently) genuine regret to (cunningly disguised) relief!

So, north-west we head, in the general direction of Dunkirk. In Ligny-en-Barrous a young lad who was with a Troupe (a travelling Circus in effect) paused during a walk with his mum and started doing backward somersaults off a road barrier. An agile and talented youngster developing his skills for a performing future. Far removed from the local boy showing off to a couple of likely looking girls. He ended up in a heap in a flower bed while over-extending his abilities doing tricks on a little push-along scooter.

I can empathise with this youngster. At school my mate and I had arranged a game of tennis with two girls. All part of growing up you know. We were about seventeen. Pete was nearly six feet and a good athlete specialising in the high hurdles. I was half a foot shorter and though not much cop at anything involving jumping, I could hold my own at most things. At the end of the first set Pete ran up and hurdled the net to go and give his preferred girl a hug. Not to be outdone I set off to do the same. Sadly, I over-estimated my abilities and snagged my leading leg on the net. My foot stooped there as the rest of me shot past and I went face-first into the shale. I was in a right old mess. Face, knees and elbows were bleeding and my smart white outfit was filthy. If I had expected my (hopefully soon to be) girlfriend to be waiting anxiously outside the local hospital after I'd been patched up, I was mistaken. I had to walk back to school alone wrapped in bandages looking like the horror element from a Hitchcock movie.

The port at Ligny shares facilities between boats and motor homes, which is not uncommon. One gregarious English camper-vanner came to chat. He lived near Gdańsk with his Polish wife (called Basha) and he was telling me what a great life he had. Poland is great, he said, adding that his house was worth a fortune and he wouldn't swap his life for anyone's. It's fabulous over there he said, you should give it a try.

'But' I pointed out, 'you live in an eastern bloc country - with a wife called Basher.'

'Yes, well,' he said after a pause, 'when you put it like that………'

We had a good laugh and I offered him a beer which he accepted and drank like a man who knows absolutely nothing about proper beer. Thankfully he didn't reciprocate with a glass of Krupnik, a Polish spirit I used to drink at the local Ukrainian club many years ago, which more often than not, would leave you a trifle unsteady for a couple of weeks.

Some large towns along the route deserve a decent port. Bar le Duc is one of these but it has poor facilities. There are pontoon spaces for perhaps 8 small boats and an alongside quay for a couple of small barges. There is plenty of unserviced bank but for such a large place, it's generally poor. It's a lovely, historic town to look around however. We witnessed a family, Mum, Dad and 3 kids, who came to sit on the grass to eat a Golden Arches take-away lunch. Not only had they to eat the filthy stuff, it was made worse when their labrador rolled in a rotting fish abandoned by a fisherman and sat down with them on their picnic blanket. The smell must have been awful. Dad dragged the dog down a slipway and told it, in no uncertain terms, to have a bath in the canal.

Attractive, serviced moorings are not common. It's not surprising that, when you come across one, like Pargny-sur-Saulx, it's full. We can't really moor against smaller cruisers because of the size and weight difference but here we came across Roger and Alison on their Czech-built barge, who invited us to raft alongside them. There was a chap here on his Dutch cruiser looking for a repair service for his bimini (that's the canvas cover supported on a stainless-steel frame over the rear deck). He'd caught it on a bridge and it definitely needed some attention. He wasn't best pleased when I started singing the Cat Steven's song, Awning has Broken - but I did put him in touch with 'Canvas Katherine', the only (and very good) bimini specialist I knew of, in St. Jean de Losne.

Then we spot a purple heron which flapped up from the reeds beside the boat as we passed. I took some amazing photos of it – so amazing that it's not easy to tell that it's actually a bird. This is the third wildlife first for me recently. Grey herons are everywhere but its purple cousin is a little thinner and, as its name cunningly suggests, is a different colour.

In Vitry-le-François I made three trips to the supermarket to buy diesel. My home-made bicycle trailer is just about up to the task and I can manage two 25-litre containers each trip. I do sway about a bit with 50 kilos of liquid in the back and don't go very fast. Invariably a traffic jam builds up behind me as mystified natives try and avoid a portly foreigner and his cobbled-together ensemble of machinery. They have an interesting fee structure in Vitry port too – 6 euros per night just to moor, if you want electricity and water it is 20 euros!

Châlons-en-Champagne is on the Canal Latéral à la Marne and the port is full, so we moor against a barge of similar size to us. The captain issued a warning telling us that the previous night, half past one in the morning in fact, he'd awoken to find a youth with a plumbers blow-lamp trying to relieve the vessel of its bicycles! Our neighbour hadn't been best pleased as this idiot could have set fire to his father-in-law's barge, not to mention the guy's young family. The port was full because they had closed the Champagne Canal, which flows south from Vitry, for dredging. I cycled up to have a look and it was a right old mess. Weed and mud everywhere as diggers filled up a rotating convoy of mucky barges who would take their load a kilometre or so to a spot where they could be unloaded by digger and the muck taken away in trucks. A fairly major operation, but at least they are maintaining the canal – it's obviously one of the major north / south routes and still used commercially so they have an incentive to keep it clear.

When we could get the internet, we had been planning where to stay for the forthcoming winter in Belgium. I'd email various ports including Veurne, Nieuwpoort, Mechelen and Diksmuide. Winter moorings, particularly the popular ones like Bruges and Ghent, tend to get booked up pretty quickly so we were surprised when all four of the ones I'd contacted were able to offer us a place. We chose Diksmuide – because it looked like a pleasant town and it was the cheapest. By coincidence the guy who replied on their behalf was called Walter Decock who we had met two or three times while pottering about France. He's a nice guy with an encyclopaedic memory of just about any place he's ever visited. We remembered each other (and he still agreed to allow us to moor at the yacht club where he is also President) and we considered this a good omen.

I needed to confirm the mooring, which meant a personal visit - to see if it was suitable for us and whether we were suitable for them. We had left our rusty old car in St. Jean de Losne so I had to get it to Belgium. I got the train from Châlons to St. Jean and then drove the six hours north to Diksmuide. I met with one of their harbourmasters and we agreed terms (which were disputed when we finally arrived on the boat – more anon!) Then I had to get the train back to Châlons. This involved a medium-fast 1½ hour trip from Diksmuide to Brussels (8 euros), a very fast TGV from Brussels to Paris (108 Euros!), a 2½ hour wait in Paris followed by another 1½ hour journey from Paris to Châlons (medium-slow, 27 Euros). Then a kilometre walk from the station to the boat – very slow. The whole trip was done in a day so I was ready for a rub-down when I got back. That wasn't available so I had a glass of Merlot instead.

Now we're heading towards Reims (pronounced Rance) via Sillery – all new stuff for us. There is a large cemetery at Sillery and walking round is an incredibly moving and humbling experience. Over 11,000 soldiers are buried here including nearly 5000 'Inconnus' (unknown) in the larger of the two ossuaries. Just a jumble of bones which were once men – it's almost too appalling to contemplate. In addition to the ossuary's, row upon row of pristine white crosses mark the final resting place of so many more brave soldiers dead before their time. It made me shiver rather because the very first cross I studied closely was one Monsieur Lucien Morilhat who died on the date of my birthday, 19th February, but 45 years earlier in 1915. As we travel through peaceful countryside from town to town, we're reminded of the great wars by distant cemeteries dotted throughout the land. The cemeteries are lovingly tended and stand out, lush green against the comparatively muted fields and forests. Each white cross the grave of a soldier now at peace, side by side with his colleagues. Men who died so we could live. When we stop and all is quiet, it's so difficult to imagine the terror and carnage that occurred here so many moons ago.

Reims port is pricey at 30+ euros per night so we moor for free just after descending the last lock before the port. It's a 300-metre stretch with good bollards, no services but perfectly fine. Reims is legendary, well-known for its Cathedral which is on Jan's wish-list of visits, in particular the lightshow that's projected onto the south wall at 10.30 each evening. It's a marvellous spectacle, not quite as good as the one in Nancy in my view, but a really memorable hour nevertheless.

We have been to Reims once before. It was a rather peculiar visit actually – because we came to scatter our mate's ashes. Our friend and neighbour in Shropshire, Terry, died miserably and suddenly following an allergic reaction to peanuts. I was away at the time but other neighbours tried to keep him alive until the ambulance arrived, sadly to no avail. He and his wife, Christine, loved France and had visited many times on holiday. They particularly liked a drop of Champagne as a special treat so what better resting place than among the vines of Champagne country. Christine hired a coach and thirty or so friends set off for a three-day trip. We stayed in a hotel in Reims and the following morning drove up into the hills to one of the many vineyards. We were high on a vine-clad promontory, right out on the point, with incredible views over the plains below. Away to our right at the bottom of the escarpment was a village where a funeral was taking place.

We held back a little as Christine moved off to privately scatter her husband's ashes among the vines. Just as she did so, as the dust settled, a lone bugle played the last post from the funeral in the valley far below. The haunting refrain floated up to us through the sunny, clear morning air. Needless to say, it was an extraordinary moment which brought many of us to tears. I'm not sure what Christine did was strictly legal but what a wonderful way to say a last goodbye.

In a way it's a peculiar feeling heading further and further away from St. Jean and our friends. Even though we have new adventures to look forward to I will always look back fondly on our mates and the things we shared. One of the last things I did together with a few of them was my peripheral involvement with the rescue of an old wooden péniche. This mini adventure is one of the reasons why we were late setting off this year. The boat is called Aster – I'll tell you a bit about her and our struggles with her.......

Peniche Aster - Magnifique

A bit of background....

The company H20, based in St. Jean de Losne, is perhaps the largest inland waterways fluvial company in France. Charles Gerard founded the company about forty years ago and is still at its head. It was Charles who came across Aster and undertook to save the ship and with it an important part of France's waterways heritage. She is the last surviving original wooden péniche (barge) in France. Built in 1951 to be horse-drawn, she plied her trade on the Canal du Nivernais firstly as a commercial carrier then, after 1972 following a major re-fit, as a trip boat. When Charles came across her she was in a sorry state, having lain abandoned for twelve years. She was slowly rotting away.

The vessel had been part of Nivernais canal life for over forty years. Sadly, the Consiel General de Nievre, who owned the vessel, was unable to pay for necessary upgrades (and ongoing maintenance) necessary after new health and safety regulations were introduced in 1999. So, it was either find a new home or scrap her. After lengthy negotiations Charles did a deal whereby Aster's ownership would be passed the Museum at St. Jean de Losne, overseen by the historical maritime organisation AQUA – for a symbolic 'purchase price' of one euro.

The boat had to be moved to St. Jean where she could be renovated and housed. This trip needed a huge amount of preparation and planning. The vessel literally had to be brought back to life. This involved basics such as getting the engines going and making sure rudimentary on-board systems worked (electric / plumbing / supplementary engines) to obtaining necessary licenses and permissions to navigate. Then find a crew who had the necessary skills and who could live together in a rickety wooden box for a week without killing each other. I was lucky enough to be invited to be involved. Having limited skills in most areas I was given a job where I could do least damage so was asked to be 'press officer'. I was responsible initially for pre-trip publicity, then for the sending of daily progress reports as we travelled (if we travelled!). These would appear on St. Jean's Museum web site and be syndicated world-wide. (Mmmmm!) So, based on those reports, here's what happened........

Pre-trip report

An advance party of five left St Jean on Thursday 29th May 2014 to begin preparations for Aster's final journey. With an estate car and a camper van both loaded to the roof with various tools and supplies we trundled through Burgundy. We were all pretty excited about our up-coming adventure - that reached fever pitch when we stopped at McDonalds in Autun. To calm down a bit we took a stroll round the remains of the nearby Roman Colosseum before continuing our journey.

Aster was in dry dock when we arrived, at around 4.00 pm, in Saint-Leger-les-Vignes, at the southern end of the Canal du Nivernais. The boat was penned in and brooding, awaiting release.

Advanced teams, more advanced than ours, had done a wonderful job cleaning and painting her hull on previous visits. Engine, generator and compressor had been overhauled and repaired and the rudder strengthened. In addition, a huge clean-up inside the boat commenced. After well over a decade of neglect, Aster was mouldy and messy, but about to be re-born.

We were wondering how and when we could move her out of dry dock when three people arrived at around 10.00 am on Friday morning. 'Now would be a good time', they said. Because soon they would be going for lunch – and that would mean a 4-hour delay. The dock was filled and Aster re-floated before we roped her gently round to her adjacent mooring.

The remaining four crew members arrived soon after that so we all had less than 24-hours to prepare. There's been talk of a five or six day trip – which seems optimistic. However long it takes, it's time for Aster to hold her head up for one last effort.

The crew has a team-bonding huddle. We democratically decide that Charles Gerard would be The Admiral (before he could elect himself to the position). So, we have a skipper with ultimate authority who would rely on everyone else. The only other elected 'officer' is Matthew Morton who would be Number Two and head tiller-man. The rest of us would be equals - enthusiastic deckhands to attend to whatever panic is most life-threatening at any given moment. Most unenviable job goes to the Systems Officer (Steve Nel) who has to get at least one of the two toilets (and poo holding tank) operational for nine fully functioning alimentary canals. The aforementioned canals are replenished by talented cooks (led by Pete Dallow, Pete D. from now on, and Helen Nel, assisted by Glenn Dallow and Patricia Gerard) who would magically conjure nourishing (and exceptional) meals from an assortment of uncoordinated donations and shrewdly-planned purchases.

While the pair who would develop into the bow crew (Peter, Bow Pete from now on, and me) nailed roofing felt to the leakiest areas of deck (this included a particularly bad spot directly above the engine batteries), Steve, with a small but select team (Pete D) was on deck dismantling, repairing and re-assembling a toilet. Disconcertingly it would only work when they blew down a pipe to prime the pump – this is all well and good when out in the open air in 'test' mode but not ideal for obvious reasons when it's been re-bolted to the floor in a dark cubicle! However, we did end up with two functioning toilets with the help of a cordless drill and some superglue. Our toilets are referred to as loo one and loo two – however, their operation is rather 'selective'. For example, we could do number ones in loo one, but not number twos. You could do number ones and number twos in loo two – except during the hours of darkness when the generator was switched off and we were strictly forbidden from doing either number ones or twos in either loo one or two – because the macerators and pumps don't work without power. The seat on loo one disintegrated at one point which put a bit of pressure on loo two, particularly at 7.15 am when the generator was started and there was a dash for the facilities. Steve also rigged up a rudimentary shower in the only space available, in a little room next to the loos, getting hot and cold water from the galley roughly 15 metres away, through newly run pipes. Due to an unfortunate technicality the main fuse panel and a number of electrical sockets were located in the shower room and despite these being taped up, we did blow the main breaker one night during a shower, so one circuit was switched off and all was well thereafter.

On the grape vine we'd heard a number of rumours regarding a local send off. We weren't sure which location was being rumoured about, either Aster's home for the previous 12 years in St.-Léger-des-Vignes or the port of Decize, a substantial town with a mayor, across the river Loire, through which we would be passing. Local dignitaries would doubtless turn up, as would journalists, but at which location or at what time, we didn't know. The Admiral decided that we would leave at 10.00 the following morning. If anyone turned up, so be it, but they would have to work round our timetable. Because there was much activity on and around the boat, we attracted lots of interest from passers-by and most seemed genuinely pleased that Aster would be saved.

She is a substantial boat at 30 metres by 5. Like a classic motor car she has few mod cons. She's not very comfortable and is generally chunky and clunky. The main cabin and bar area is quite respectable as that's where day-trippers were entertained in days gone by. From a distance she's a wonderful, grand old lady but if you look closely, she's world-weary. The paintwork is shabby and (whisper it) there's a touch of rot here and there. The roof leaks a bit, but the sun is out, so who cares. But despite her rumpled, wrinkled coat, she is magnificent.

The crew are an experienced bunch having piloted in a wide variety of craft over many years (including aeroplanes). Aster however is something else altogether. For example, the propeller is attached to the rear of the rudder and wiser folk than me 'have never seen the like'. Apparently in French it's known as a 'sculling' propeller - in any event it will doubtless take a bit of getting used to. We had the expertise of local man, Monsieur Cretier, who had skippered Aster during her passenger-carrying days, to call on. He was heartbroken to see his beloved ship leave for the last time and seemed a little reluctant to pass on his experience just so we could take her away. But despite his distress he was a big help. However, he refused our offer to pilot Aster on her final voyage.

By Friday evening we felt as prepared as we would ever be so went for a 'shake-down cruise' in the basin. The idea was to turn Aster round so we faced the lock in preparation for (a smooth and graceful) departure the following morning in front of the TV cameras. All went well till the engine stalled when changing from forward to reverse gear. A gear change is accomplished by lowering the revs and heaving a large steel lever forward or back. It was soon running again but you don't want 60 tonnes of boat moving in either direction without an engine. We moored up ready for next day's departure and anchors were lashed fore and aft in case of another failure, the front one so heavy it took four of us to hump it into position. If we ever have to lob it out in an emergency, that is where it will stay because there's no way we could get it back.

We were a little unsure how Aster would behave when we set off but if Pete D's magnificent bolognaise we had the eve of departure was representative of what was to come, cuisine was one area we would have no worries.

The voyage begins

Saturday 31st May 2014

Aster was dressed for her final journey. She actually looked very presentable from the waist down, it's the top-sides that are rather tatty. Banners, flags and bunting were hung to jazz her up and disguise the mottled bits. The crew of nine, dressed in bright yellow T-shirts and black caps, buzzed about like a swarm of nervous, happy bees. France 3 TV was there, as were a number of journalists. We chatted to them and other guests who we encouraged on board and tried to stop them dislodging any rotten bits or tripping over our red roofing felt. Some guests were very knowledgeable about the workings of our boat, some had seen her plying her trade on The Nivernais as a passenger trip boat and many others showed a genuine interest in the layout and history of Aster. In fact, it's fair to say that many bystanders knew much more about the boat than the crew did. Sadly, not one member of the crew was French.

Whichever way you look at it, the restoration and preservation of Aster will be an expensive business, the intention being to fund it by donations and any sponsorship that can be found. We'd done some merchandising and our T-shirt stall on the quay was doing steady business – but it was time to go.

The DK 3 Baudoiun engine rumbled into life, the electricity shore line was uncoupled, mooring lines untied and we were on our own. We reversed back into the pound and prepared to attack our first lock. With the Admiral at the helm, we were off.

We had various guests on board including the President and Curator of the Musée de la Batellerie and journalist Phillipe Menager from Fluvial Magazine.

The lock was circled by well-wishers as we approached. Thankfully and skilfully The Admiral and First Mate piloted Aster straight and true. We waved for the cameras and acknowledged horns hooted from the nearby road. The lock emptied, the gates opened and Aster left The Nivernais canal, after more than sixty years, for the last time.

Following a final, brief flirt with the iconic River Loire, we ascend a lock into the port of Decize where another group of well-wishers wave us on our way, including old friends from St. Jean, Roger and Jenni from the boat Manjana. Through the port, up one more lock, we join the Canal Lateral al la Loire and head south towards Chalon-sur-Saone and the junction of the River Saone.

Piloting Aster is easy, almost anyone can do that. Piloting her with any degree of accuracy on a twisty canal into lock entrances barely bigger than the boat is an art which takes skill and nerve – particularly if the wind blows. The Admiral and First Mate share responsibility for the driving. Fine course adjustments are made by manipulating the main rudder, the bow rudder and speed. Main rudder and speed we all know about but the bow rudder is not something you come across every day and is worthy of explanation.

It is an interesting piece of equipment which, when we arrived initially, had been hanging idle down the side of the boat having been dismantled years ago. The underwater section is a large, heavy fin attached to a short shaft, which in turn is attached to a chain. We'd had to haul the shaft up through a tube in the bottom of the boat by means of the chain until the fin was immediately below the bow of the boat. The attached shaft protruded 60 centimetres up through the hull into the bar area. Here it is temporarily secured by means of a steel pin inserted through a pre-drilled hole in the shaft. A permanent collar, which prevents the assembly disappearing through the bottom of the boat was then attached to the shaft and the safety pin removed. A further shaft was fed down from the deck above through another tube and attached to the top of the rudder-shaft in the bar. Finally, what resembles a huge set of bicycle handlebars is fixed to the top shaft on deck. Two trailing ropes, one attached to each end of the handlebars were fed back to the rear deck (15 metres away) from where the bow-rudder is operated. Quite simply, pulling the ropes turns the rudder below the bow and helps steer the front of the boat.

Although this is a serious business we do have plenty of laughs and mickey-taking – particularly after a manoeuvre has been successfully completed – or not.

The person driving can control the main tiller and throttle but realistically needs the assistance of at least one crew member to operate the bow rudder and gear lever – on tricky stretches we usually used two extra pairs of hands – with others keeping a close eye. This is where communication comes in. It shouldn't be a problem for the steerer to issue instructions to those operating at the rear of the vessel, but the pair at the bow are nearly 30 metres away – further than most of us can run! The bow pair need to know the skipper's intentions to prepare fenders, make minor adjustments to the bow rudder or warn the steerer of misalignments when approaching a lock.

There are many forms of communication on board – a hissing, beeping melange of individual units ranging from 2-way radios and mobile phones to the internet, but there were times when Bow Pete and I at the bow were forced to use our prodigious psychic powers to figure out what was intended. Under our professional names of Psychic Simon and Gandolfo the Unpredictable we would 'tune in'. Usually we could pick something up (particularly when the 2-ways were tuned to the correct channel) but occasionally we were unable to pick up the skippers (sometimes unspoken) instructions. On such occasions we would inevitably thunder into another lock wall – and we would stoically take the blame.

Another difficulty (related to me subsequently by a member of the bow-rudder steering crew at the rear) was that The Admiral and First mate use differing terminology. The First Mate's instructions were invariably clear and polite, spoken with the calm authority of an airline captain informing his terrified passengers that number one engine had just failed, but not to worry. His refined tone of voice never wavered no matter what mess he was in. 'Bow rudder left please'. 'Bow rudder right'. Bow rudder amidships'. 'And, done. Thank you'. Measured tones of natural authority drifted forward to us on the bow - just before another 200-year-old chunk of stonework parted company from a bridge.

The Admiral used another method and issued his instructions quietly, in a crisp deliberate manner. 'Bow rudder right'. Bow rudder left'. 'Bow rudder neutral' - and this is where the problems started. Hearing the word neutral, the First Mate would leap for the gear selector and crunch the gear box into neutral thereby rendering the craft temporarily powerless. Even if the engine didn't stall, the resulting delay would muck up a manoeuvre to the extent where a re-alignment was necessary, meaning a reverse back up the canal before a fresh attack.

Peter and I laughed a lot but took our fair share of flak from the stern – often for fabricated reasons, but judging by the laughter we could hear, there was plenty of fun being had at the back too.

We took the micky but I have to say that we all had great respect for the way the steerers handled the boat. I watched both The Admiral and First Mate at close quarters while they drove and I, like the rest of the crew I'm sure, was mightily impressed. Well done gentlemen.

As I've mentioned the old engine was a little temperamental and had a tendency to stall – 10 times on the first day would you believe, before a technique was worked out to minimize the possibility. When changing gear with the engine in tick-over, it often stalled. So, we increased the revs a little and crashed the gearbox quickly into gear rather than feathering it in. To begin with, these stalls were alarming for everyone, particularly when entering a lock when we had to slow and stop the boat on ropes alone - but we came to expect the unexpected. Bear in mind that we are still on the first day – the learning curve was long and steep.

Then we had a major problem with the gearbox overheating, so hot in fact that it smoked. Slowing down seemed to alleviate the problem but we were finally forced to stop. We were really worried that the trip would be over before it had barely begun – or at the very least result in a severe delay. We moored up on a very isolated stretch and the mechanics among the crew investigated. Astonishingly the fault was identified as a piece of cloth. This had been tied to a steel bar as a warning to stop people bashing their heads on it. The cloth had slipped down to a linkage which prevented it extending fully, only by a small margin, but enough to mean that the clutch plates couldn't engage properly. The rag was removed and the problem solved – we were very, very lucky.

While some of the crew were messing around with rags, others performed a rescue. Just as we were mooring up a young deer jumped into the canal nearby. It was unable to get out as the sides were lined with steel piling which extended about 40 centimetres above water level. A following hire boat had stopped a hundred or so metres back preventing the poor animal from swimming away. Pete D and I took our long boarding plank with the intention of placing it in the canal as a means of escape. The plank is a very heavy thing and as we approached the deer we dropped it – largely because we are so feeble! The deer was so startled by the noise that it leapt out of the water and disappeared into the trees. Pity really, we'd talked about getting a BBQ.

Despite all the problems we made approximately 26 kilometres and did 9 locks on a truncated first day. That first night we stayed at Rosiere, Écluse 10.

The second day was much smoother and the engine stalled only twice, on neither occasion in difficult situations.

It has taken the 'Admiral' and his crew some time to figure out the vagaries of the old engine and gearbox. Thankfully there are experienced people on board, both mechanically and from a boat handling perspective, on whom he can call.

We have received much good will en route, many people waving, hooting horns and chatting at locks. The towpath is busy with cyclists and walkers and Aster has been photographed hundreds of times. There is a photographic record of the trip on the St Jean de Losne Museum's web site at: www.musee-saintjeandelosne.com

Pete and Glenn Dallow took around 1600 photographs from which they created the on-line collection. The weather to date has been warm and sunny so there are some wonderful photos of Aster, her crew, well-wishers and the picturesque canals and rivers.

The second night (1st June) we stayed at a petite Halte Nautique at Molinet, near Digoin having travelled a very respectable 37 kilometres including 9 locks. The days are long and it can be very hard work, particularly for the steerers, who need to concentrate. Manipulating the tiller is also pretty physical, particularly on twisty stretches or when manoeuvring near locks and bridges. Consequently, at the end of what are 10 or 11-hour days we are rather weary. A good meal helps, Helen's Chicken Basque was one of a few delicious meals – the remainder being BBQs. Pete D. rigged up a music system that played throughout the boat, including speakers on deck. We relaxed to an eclectic mix including Pink Floyd, Janis Joplin, The Eagles and Leonard Cohen.

Lights out 10.00 pm. Five of the nine stay on board and we retire to the floor to sleep. Yes, floor. Four of us sleep on various inflatable beds and one on a steel fold-up contraption (that we suspect last saw service as a captain's berth on a 747 - though that was denied). There are 3 of us in the saloon and 2 in the bar. The bow crew were particularly ill-prepared. On the first evening my mattress sprung a leak so within a few minutes I was lying directly on the polished wooden floor. (Thank you David Ross for supplying us with a spare mattress!) Bow Pete has the least impressive 'self-inflating' mattress ever invented. In the blink of an eye, it magically expands from the thickness of a sheet of aluminium foil to the thickness of paper kitchen towel. In the morning most of us need to perform a series of extremely unpleasant 'loosening-up' exercises just to get to the bathroom. Of the remaining four crew members, two sleep in their camper van while the others merely disappear during the hours of darkness – to where, nobody knows.

The crew, apart from a few minor injuries, are generally fit and well. The most serious injury occurred when Bow Pete tried to demolish a stone bridge with his cranium. Fortunately, the bridge only sustained minor damage and we were able to continue. The sun is strong and there are a few painfully burnt appendages – there is no shade on deck.

Day three saw us depart Molinet at 8.15am, much to the disgust of those still eating breakfast, in order to arrive in Digoin Port at 9.00 am and a rendezvous with the deputy mayor of Digoin, Mme. Nicole Georges. We were delighted to welcome her aboard with her colleague and she showed great enthusiasm for Project Aster wishing us well both for the remainder of our trip and for the future of the project. Fortunately, she was so engrossed in her short trip that, when asked to sit down to avoid injury on a low bridge, she didn't notice that she was sitting on a pair of underpants. They had been washed (by a nameless member of the crew) and were drying on the chair in the sun. Actually, I admit, they were mine. Although the practice may be quite common in Town Halls around the world, this is the first time that I have had a Deputy Mayor sit on my underpants. Residents of the port, unaware of the 'nether-wear-happenings' on board, stood by and waved us on our way.

The sound of our engine is one that turns heads, the 3-cylinder motor thumps out a steady rhythm - 'PUM pum pum – PUM pum pum – PUM pum pum', The noise echoes off buildings and trees and provides a steady, reassuring heartbeat (except when it stalls). Cyclists, walkers, car drivers and truckers all wave, smile and give us a thumbs-up. How can you not smile when you see a grand old lady chugging down the canal crewed by a group of misfits dressed in yellow shirts and black caps.

En route to Paray-le-Monial we hit a submerged object so stopped to check for damage to the propeller. This involved six people. The Admiral led the operation while standing on the propeller itself (which had been raised out of the water by means of a winch) to see if it had been bent. The remaining five people stood by, muttering unhelpful advice. Fortunately, the propulsion system was passed fit and we continued through Paray where they were in the process of erecting acre upon acre of marquees for the annual ingress of pilgrims. Despite being pilgrimless at present, it makes quite a sight as the town prepares to welcome hundreds of thousands of visitors.

Today we cruised 36 kilometres ascending 11 locks having travelled from 8.15 am until 7.00 pm when we moored at Genelard. We passed one single boat all day and were shouted at by another. The vocal gentleman was ratty that we didn't have our VHF tuned into his personal frequency so we could advise him of our time of arrival. We told him we didn't have a VHF – so that fuelled his ire! Other boats just stayed out of our way, fearful of meeting us in the narrow channel. One such boat was Ad Locem. Owners Henry and Steph, known for their thrift, actually handed us a parcel for delivery to St. Jean, our destination, as we passed, as if we were the Pony Express. Well, not quite – the ponies of yesteryear have been replaced by an engine and express is woefully inaccurate.

Day 4 we departed Genelard at 9.00 am aiming to travel to Montchanin.

A relatively uneventful day mechanically - thankfully. The only chaotic scene of note was the bow crew trying to erect a BBQ. It came in many assorted pieces, including lengths of steel tube, nuts and bolts and couple of wheels. We had to stand on the instructions to prevent them blowing away in the stiff wind and somehow managed to get a couple of tubes mixed up so the wheels ended up on the wrong legs – much to the amusement of the Admiral. Thus, rather than pushing it pram style you had to lift up one side and crab sideways with it – perfect for moving it down corridors we reasoned.

Actually, there was another episode worthy of note. We have a camper van and two cars with us. These are used for sleeping (camper) and shopping. All three vehicles need to be leap-frogged down the route so at least one is available at our daily port of destination. This morning three crew members (who, to maintain their anonymity and dignity, will be known only as A, B and C) set off in one car. 'A' was dropped at a supermarket, where the campervan and second car were parked, to do the shopping while B and C went to top up the car with fuel a few kilometres away. There was a 'slight mishap with fuel types' rendering the car temporarily immobile! This necessitated B and C having to thumb a lift back to A where the shopping and other vehicles awaited. Unfortunately, B and C, although attractive and dressed in fetching summer attire, and on a busy road, failed to attract a lift and arrived back with

A on foot thirty minutes later! 'A' was very amused, as were the remaining letters of the alphabet when later appraised of the happenings.

The Canal lateral a La Loire became the Canal du Centre in Digoin. We are now moored near Montchanin, close to the first descending lock on the summit pound of the Canal du Centre.

Genelard is a pretty, peaceful place with ideal mooring facilities for a big barge. Arriving in Montchanin last evening at 6.45 pm the Admiral (on advice from his underlings) ignored a beautifully maintained VNF mooring near a leisure lake and parked alongside a thicket of nettles below a TGV railway line. Fortunately, a previous explorer had unearthed some bollards in the undergrowth so we could safely moor, at one with nature, in the jungle. The last of those pesky trains roared by at 10.20 pm so by the time everybody was utterly exhausted we could retire to the floor to sleep.

Today we managed 33 kilometres and 16 locks.

It's day five, 6.20 in the morning and the first TGV of the day blasts by overhead.

We leave Montchanin at 9.00 am. These were our first down-hill locks and presented quite a challenge to The Admiral. They are tricky because it is very difficult to 'spot' the exact lock entrance from the rear of a big boat that has a high, wide bow. Aster handles very well generally. As I've said it's a tricky balance managing the throttle, gear lever, the enormous tiller and the bow rudder but even if we get this right, things happen slowly so a change of course has to be anticipated. The tiller handle incidentally has been made even longer by two lashed-together broom-handles that have been added as an extension. Although the arrangement looks a bit peculiar, it is useful should someone want to sweep the rear deck during a quiet spell.

Today it is raining – persistently throughout the morning, then blustery showers. Our real enemy is the wind, and at one point we experienced a really nasty squall on approach to a lock. A terrific mini-storm, torrential rain and strong wind that that thankfully only lasted five minutes or so. We were literally blown sideways into the bank. No damage thank goodness, just a delay as we reversed back up the canal and tried again.

To make things easier for the Admiral (who had taken responsibility for getting us through the down-hill locks) we had two 'point-men' on shore who stood each side of the lock entrance to give the skipper a sight marker and count down the remaining metres to the lock from ten to zero via 2-way radios. For the first 11 locks bicycles were used to accompany the boat lock to lock, then a car via public roads when the towpath ran out! The bow crew (Bow Pete and I) usually stood point on the lock's entrances. It turns out that we were no use whatsoever – the Admiral didn't bother telling us because he 'thought we needed to feel involved'.

Anybody seeing us from the shore witness a relaxed and efficient crew piloting our temperamental old barge through beautiful Burgundy with time for a chat and a wave to passers-by. But from within the boat, it can be a different story – basics need to be addressed. For example, the engine room can be a problem area – engine re-starts after a stall or insufficient pressure in the compressed air cylinder, which is used to start the engine. These problems need to be tackled urgently. Calmness and know-how are vital to sort things out and thankfully the well-oiled crew can manage the problems. (Well-oiled in this context means smooth and efficient rather than pickled! Although it's fair to say that on occasion some of us were more pickled than smooth and efficient). Today the black waste tank was full to the brim (there is no gauge to ascertain fluid levels) and the discharge pump failed to work. The Systems Officer and his cohorts had to open an inspection hatch on the tank and rig up pumps and pipes to keep our waste system operational. Basic requirements, but necessary.

We arrive at Chagny at 7.30 pm having covered 29 kilometres and descended 23 locks. We are making quicker progress than any of us imagined. Entering the port, the wind was howling so getting the boat to the shore and tying up safely tested everyone to the limit. It is so easy to lose control in a relatively small space in a strong wind. Praise of the highest order must go the First Mate for guiding us in safely.

Today (day 6) we will stop for lunch in Fragnes before descending the 10-metre lock onto the River Saone and beginning the last leg of the journey to St. Jean. This evening we will moor on the river, the exact location to be determined by our progress, but the intention is to be at or near Écuelles.

The rain has stopped, thank goodness – because Aster does dribble rather through windows, decks and gunwales. We used the cardboard box from our recently purchased BBQ to cover a leaky hatch that was dripping down the stairs on to our First Mate's bed!

There was a delay this morning – the young lockkeeper arrived twenty minutes late, apologised, then said he would be even later because he had to go and get the key to open the lock. We can't believe how quiet it is. Quite extraordinarily, in the previous 48-hours, we have seen only one other moving boat. This morning as we wait for the lock there is one in front and three behind – it's like coming back to the present having spent so much time alone in the wonderful countryside with our dear barge. It's busier now due to the hire-boats bases at Saint-Leger-sur-Dheune and Chagney.

We had a mechanical near catastrophe today. Our rudder and tiller arm bounce and buck because the propeller is attached to the bottom of the rudder. When the tiller is hard over to one side (when manoeuvring for a lock for example) you may need to change from forward to reverse gear or change the speed of the engine. This may mean letting go of the tiller arm briefly. When one of our pilots did this earlier today, the rudder took on a life of its own and settled in a position at nearly 90 degrees to the stern of the boat. We were told while being instructed in the operation of the boat that 30 degrees is the limit because it puts too much pressure on the universal joint connecting the gearbox to the propeller shaft. There were sickening grinding noises before the engine stalled and we all thought that our trip had come to an end there and then. But no, testament to the strength and resilience of the machinery (and stubbornness of our dear old boat), everything worked perfectly when the engine was re-started. Once again the Gods were kind.

A gentleman approached us at a lock. He was a retired journalist who used to write about the Canal du Nivernais and Aster. He had heard about our adventure and come to offer some of his personal photographs for our archives. The more we travel, the more we realize how much Aster has touched people's lives in one way or another.

We were all wearing our yellow and black 'wasp' t-shirts when we arrived at Fragnes, a pretty little village with immaculate Haulte Nautique. Yellow is not the colour to wear when travelling through the corn fields as we get covered in tiny black flies. Thankfully the metropolis of Fragnes was fly-free as we welcomed guests aboard, some friends, others strangers, all showing genuine interest in Aster. We are constantly reminded that to renovate and maintain her, money will be needed.

We had called in here to do our diplomatic bit with the local dignitaries as well as trying to flog a few T-shirts. Sales in Fragnes were 'steady rather than stratospheric', but another few Euros went into the fund. Those we sold were thanks primarily to Patricia's persuasive powers. However, her job was made considerably easier because the T-shirts were being modelled by each member of the perfectly proportioned crew (?) who stood, high on the deck above, like a collection of Greek Gods against an azure sky!!

Anyhow, while Patricia was counting our takings, we prepared to depart. The bow crew had noticed a nasty tree stump protruding into the canal, substantial enough to have damaged Aster's wooden hull. We retrieved the boat pole from the cabin roof and heaved the bow away from the shore into a perfect position for a smooth getaway, thereby avoiding said root. The engine roared but for some reason, known only to The Admiral, he set off in reverse! The bow crew, a little perplexed by this turn of events, then had to scramble to get a line ashore when the engine stalled as the rear deckers changed from reverse to forward gear. Aster was now careering backwards towards a boat moored to our stern. It was more luck than judgement that one of our crew members was still ashore and able to place our rope over a bollard so we could bring her to a stop. It took a little time to run the compressor to re-charge the pressurized cylinder required to re-start the main engine, so we moored up again. We could have left the T-shirt stall out for a while longer. Having said that, anyone wishing to be associated with a boat that had just performed such a shambolic manoeuvre would probably be better off spending their money on psychiatric evaluation rather than a T-shirt. (To be fair to The Admiral, reversing off is standard procedure for large péniches. They back off before swinging the bow back on line. The bow crew stoically took the blame for this latest mess.

Down the 10-metre-deep lock we entered the channel that gave us access to the River Saone. Here our escort boat awaited. Bateau Cornelia Helena, skippered by Ruedi Kung, was bedecked with colourful flags - a wonderful sight in the afternoon sun. Ruedi used to skipper steam passenger boats on the Swiss lakes, is an engine restorer and highly knowledgeable engineer – an ideal escort we are lucky to have with us. They would track us during the approximate 10-hour journey upriver to St. Jean. We were obliged to have a support boat on the river as a condition of our insurance cover - just in case anything went awry.

We didn't reach our target at Écuelles because the canal had been twisty, the wind difficult and there were many more boats about. So instead, we moored at Gurgey, roughly two hours up the river. We appreciated the boat-shuffling of those already there to enable us to tie for the night (although one or two had to be 'encouraged' to move! Imagine the horror of these moored boats when our huge hulk rumbled up and demanded to share their mooring). Ruedi came along side us and an eleven-hour day came to an end – at least it did three hours later after out 3rd consecutive BBQ!

Today we cruised approximately 33 kilometres and 12 locks.

Tomorrow will be our last day – regretfully.

We left at 8.30 am. Untying was a time-consuming business because we were perched on the end of the floating pontoons overhanging by half a boat length. We had a lengthy rope attached to long-disused bollard up on the bank 20 metres away. This was countered by a boat pole jammed in the riverbed and lashed to a bollard on the boat to keep the bow away from the bank. Further ropes were tied to the concrete quay to which the pontoons were attached and others to inadequate cleats on the pontoon itself.

We'd taken on guests for our final day, all supporters and enthusiasts for Project Aster. These included Danielle Moullet, curator of the Musée de la Batellerie de Saint-Jean-de-Losne, former barge skippers, journalists and a musician who writes and sings songs about the waterways. Our guests more than doubled our number. It was fabulous to see the support but sad in a way that this was the final day of a great adventure for the nine crew members who had laughed, worked and suffered together depending on whether things had gone well or badly.

Anybody who expressed an interest steered the boat for a spell on the wide river, crew and guests alike. For the inexperienced it was a thrill to be handling this wonderful, historic barge. She may be rough around the edges but she is still a proud (albeit on occasion temperamental) old lady who has allowed mere mortals to lead her on. For others, for example bargees with decades of experience handling large boats, it was less the size, more the nostalgia and history attached to Aster that I hope gave them a reminder of their skills and way of life.

But throughout, whoever was at the helm, somehow Aster was always in charge. She could always spring a surprise. We have to remember that she has not moved for well over a decade – she is entitled to be grumpy at times.

Ascending the river lock at Écuelles was rather traumatic. The fore and aft wash of the incoming water tested Asters bollards to their limits, particularly at the stern where they actually lifted slightly each time substantial strain was put on them as the water surged. Those on the rear deck feared the whole bollard assembly may part company with the ship. Our escort boat, Cornelia Helena, was further back in the lock and actually snapped a bow line during one surge.

It is a breezy day, cooling, as the temperature reached the high twenties. The huge French Tricolour snapped at its staff from the stern, as did the hand-sewn 'Aster' flag on the bow. She made a steady 7 kilometres per hour against a slight current, pretty impressive really as Aster was previously operated on the Canal Du Nivernais and rarely as fast as that or for such a sustained period. The gearbox throughout the trip became extremely hot and engine oil needed to be topped up from time to time but she ploughed on as the reassuring throb of the old engine thumped back echoes from riverside trees.

The pivotal role in crewing Aster is naturally the person at the helm at any given moment but everybody played a part. Crewing Aster is not a one-person job – her 3 motors (main engine, generator and compressor) only run if we tend them and she will only go where we tell her to. If we bump a wall, we all take a share of the blame – it's certainly not the boat's fault.

Danielle Moullet gave Patricia some candles before the start of our trip. One was lit every morning and left to burn throughout the day in the saloon to keep us safe. Well, it worked, we made it.

Motoring under the bridge and past the quay at St. Jean de Losne was an experience I shall never forget as horns were blown and people waved and took photos. I have spoken to two other crew members who shed tears, 'tough guys' the three of us – I didn't need to speak with the remaining crew.

Aster was piloted on this final stretch by Jeanine Hornez, a former bargee now in her eighties. She operated a commercial freycinet (a 39-metre barge) single-handed for many years – while bringing up two children. It was a privilege to welcome her on board for our final day and 'like riding a bike' she piloted the boat straight and true.

Our welcome in St. Jean de Losne was amazing and immensely moving - I hope Aster is now assured that we mean her no harm.

She took centre stage at a ceremony held on the quay at St. Jean, namely the Blessing of the Boats where a bishop says a prayer and sprinkles holy water over any boat taking part. For two days we offered visitors guided tours. Many newcomers came to say hello but also many people associated with her past.

Aster is currently in the Écluse Ancienne (Old lock) three kilometres down the river. A tarpaulin has been erected over the whole boat supported by a steel frame. This will enable restoration work to get under way out of the weather. Although initially Aster was going to be housed in a purpose-built tank on shore, there is now talk of her being used for river trips and functions. It would be marvellous if it came about because this dear old boat deserves another life.

New Loo and a Road Trip

When we first bought our barge, Vrouwe Johanna, she was in rather a sorry state. We have worked hard over the years to reach the point where we are proud of her. She's been a great home for us. The Ford engine, although forty-plus years old, has never let us down once – indeed turns heads a bit with its grumbling exhaust. She's an old boat, built in 1905, and as with anything of that age, she needs nurturing. Of course (as with anything that has complicated systems) the odd thing does go wrong but we've learned enough about her to fix problems.

We've just had to replace a battery charger for example – thankfully not the big Victron that charges our big bank of domestic batteries, no this is the 'just out of warranty' fancy little thing that charges the engine starter battery. Seems it objected either to the intense heat (40+ degrees) or the fact that we had to stop / re-start the engine dozens of times on the upper reaches of the Marne Canal due to our water filters getting clogged with weed. We had to stop every lock (and there are plenty) over one stretch. In fact, there was so much garbage in one lock that we actually bow-hauled the boat out otherwise we would have been clogged before we even got out of the lock.

In the early days I lost count of the sleepless nights worrying about this problem or that balls-up, sometimes wondering what on earth we'd done. But now, thankfully, problems are few and if anything crops up, we just tackle it.

Yes, these days there are moments of great peace when fluffy little bunnies float through our consciousness and the problems of life are a world away. A nirvana where you achieve an imperturbable stillness of mind. Like a place of dreams conjured from the imagination of a contented science fiction writer floating through time on his ship of illicit substances - well, you get the idea. Mind you, I normally find peace when I've consumed enough wine to drown a small sheep and am having a nap.

There are moments of excitement – like when two chaps were attacked by another with an Axe in Clamecy on The Nivernais canal and I performed some rudimentary first aid on the victims.

There have been moments of intense joy – but not since I was in my early teens.

Last evening, I was sitting on the blunt end, with a glass of something extremely ordinaire, contemplating what else might go awry, when I watch a sleek, graceful TGV slither out of a station. Oh, for something sleek and graceful! (In addition to Jan).

Tomorrow we are heading for....well, who knows?

Of course during the renovations you don't necessarily get everything right first time. For example, I'd installed a multi-fuel stove early on as keeping warm is one of the essentials. It's not too difficult if you follow safety parameters but quite time-consuming. Building hearth, fire surround, flue, etc. takes a bit of know-how but, time allowing, most people could probably manage it. Then we decided to re-hash the lounge which meant moving it again. Bad planning! One early modification was born of necessity. My mate Alan, who is six-foot-four and a substantial item generally, came to help with some of the early renovations. Our sea toilet is positioned with it's rear against the side of the boat. Because of the shape of the cabin side, it means you can only raise the lid about three-quarters of the way back. The room is small, so much so that Alan, when seated, couldn't get the door shut because his knees were in the way. 'Bloody hell,' he said, 'it's the first time I've had to go side-saddle!' So, I put a hinge in the toilet seat – literally chopped it across the centre so now it folds back under the gunwale. Big Al can now go without his knees poking out into the kitchen. I've since installed another loo in the shower room. This one is a sleek, modern macerator model, more suited to refined guests (and Jan!). While fitting it I was unsure about the waste-pipe exit. This is because it is above the water line. After all you can't go drilling holes below water-level while the boat is in the water! A friend of ours, who used to own a 34-metre boat, had four such toilets on board which all exited above the water line and he never had a problem with them. Should anyone in the future want to re-plumb the waste below water-level I have installed an anti-syphon valve. But of course, we had to test our new loo. Not so bad for number ones but I was worried that the 'evacuation' of number twos would entail hurling unmentionables across the port. The only way to test this was to do a 'visual'. This meant Jan flushing the loo while I watched from outside. Unfortunately, just at the wrong juncture, Jan got 'bunged up' so it was three days before we could perform the test.

'Right', she said eventually, in a state of some excitement and relief, 'I'm ready.'

I dashed outside to witness proceedings only to find a family of four eating lunch on their rear deck right across the pontoon.

I ran back inside. 'Hang on!' I shouted.

'Can't' she yelled back.

Luckily we got away with it. The machinery worked flawlessly and next door's lunch was (relatively) undisturbed.

Before we leave France I'll tell about another little adventure we had – a road trip........

Barging is wonderful but not great if you want to visit our friends in their house on a hill north of Toulouse or the Swiss mountains – which we did. So, we decided to spend the equivalent of two month's boat diesel money on an economy trip in our economy car. Nothing lavish you understand, basically living cheap and trying to scrounge off friends on the way round – whom we would repay with witty repartee (a debt we would find very difficult to honour) and the promise of a trip on our boat (which we could honour).

So, by way of a side-track, here's an account of our mini tour.........

We are in the storm. Not below it, right in it. Nearly a thousand metres up a mountain on a twisty, flooded road - visibility is 10 metres. Thankfully I had recently installed two new tyres on the front – despite the fact that they were overpriced and they'd failed to balance the wheels properly, at least we had a chance of sticking to the road on the steep descent. The new tyres stood out rather on our old car – like putting new shoes on a tramp.

Two hours south of St. Jean we arrive at our inn in our beloved steed, a Peugeot of some age with a rusty bonnet. Tonight we are staying at Les Liards which is an 'auberge écologique'. It is a kilometre outside the tiny village of Egliseneuve les Liards in the natural regional parc of Livradois Forez. If you were to combine all those long words with the splendid isolation of the village, the Sat Nav would come back with, 'I beg your pardon?

Unsurprisingly, the place is deserted. Come to think of it we haven't seen a single person for about twenty minutes – perhaps the whole region is deserted. But no, Father and son are hacking away at a hedge with 'implements' up the hillside. When they silence their brush-cutters the peace is absolute until a rumble of thunder from the departing storm booms across the landscape. We are in the region of The Auvergne - volcano country. Sleeping, tree-clad cones adorn the distant panorama. A drama enhanced as shafts of watery sunlight pierce the dispersing storm-clouds, like spotlights on God's stage. The vista is awe-inspiring.

The volcanoes last erupted around 6000 years ago and continue to snooze – a good job as our auberge is perched on the slopes of one.

We found it on the internet having searched 'B & B', 'Vichy' and 'cheap'. My co-pilot didn't want 'Formula' hotels during our little adventure where the shower, loo, basin and bed are all fashioned from one lump of fibreglass, no, she would rather root out individual, quirky establishments that are obliged to look after you. If they don't make an effort, one ugly slash of the keyboard can undo years of trade-boosting internet reviews.

Walter, a fit, leathery-skinned Dutchman, is our host and apologizes for chairs upturned on tables in the oak-beamed, two-storey main reception room. He explains that we are the only guests (though he was full last week) and he hadn't spotted our booking email until lunchtime that day. Nevertheless, he was very welcoming and showed us our room which was 'Zebra-themed' - testament to his travels in Africa. Everything was black and white and it smelled faintly musty, like a zebra hoof perhaps. No dinner was available so we had a picnic in the guest lounge. My wife, Jan, is a great picnic maker. Even the shortest trips are prepared for with ham sandwiches and a flask – I've renamed her Jan butty and we are often thankful for her road-trip creations.

The following morning, on the patio outside the breakfast room (which I share with Walter) two peahens sit on nearby tables and a peacock parades his wonderful tail feathers. Unfortunately, his back is to us so we have a bird's eye view of him pooping on the patio. Breakfast is organic, including different varieties of home-made bread and pine-resin jam, which is a first for me. Ducks and chickens wander around the homestead largely unhindered, a source of aesthetic delight - and food, at which time they become a little more hindered.

The auberge was a good start but the trip went downhill briefly on day two because it found us having a light lunch and a nap in Carrefour's car park in Aurillac. We'd had to re-enter the real world – terrific jam to traffic jam via 2-hours of stunning scenery on roads up to 1100 metres high and through a cherry orchard. The latter happened-upon as we once again tuned the Sat-Nav to 'shortest route' taking us off piste. Row after row of cherry trees ran up hill and down dale. The odd car was parked in the shade here and there as cherry-pickers reaped their bounty.

Caylus is our destination in Tarn-et-Garonne, or more accurately the hamlet of Lassalle 4 km north, home to our friends Kim and Andy. We are staying in their Gite for a few days and would have sunbathed and swum in their pool if it weren't 20 degrees too cold. Instead, we lit the log-burner and fired up the electric blanket. We lived near each other in Shropshire before they moved south with their two boys. They both work from home. Andy, an archaeologist who uses nearby Toulouse Airport for his travels and Kim is a fitness trainer who has 'clients' come to their on-site gym fashioned from an old barn. She tortures people with oriental-sounding exercise routines and an assortment of injury-threatening accessories.

We'd not been there long when Andy was called out on an emergency mission to help a nearby local. Her Land Rover Discovery was dead so I went along to offer pithy advice (from a position of some technical weakness). Her husband was away and the lady was struggling in her isolated house. We poked about in the rain and found a battery lead disconnected. That was the easy bit – then we were invited in for coffee. The kitchen was not the tidiest and was a tad pongy so we weren't off to the best start. Then a big dalmation-type dog ambled in. It was a lethargic creature, spotty and muddy. It also had a penchant for testicle-sniffing and became a bit over-familiar. The only place I could find solace was by standing with my nether regions against the arm of the sofa. My little plan worked perfectly until mother sat down with her large, grumbling 3-year-old boy and began to breast-feed him right under my nose. This male lump was lying across her lap like a big, dozy carp – the like of which you see on the front of fishing magazines, making noises like a partially blocked sluice. The dog wandered off in search of parts new. Andy, standing over by the window, was highly amused by this state of affairs and smirked right up to the point where the dog chose him for his next investigation.

The Saturday of our stay saw Kim host a 'Fit Camp' where a dozen ladies paid to put themselves through various tortures accompanied by booming 'dance' music. Due to a bit of a planning oversight the clients bought their kids with them and it was our 'job' (Jan, Andy and me) to entertain them while the Mums were jigging about in the nearby shed. There were twelve kids aged between one and fifteen whose behaviour and bodily functions ranged from perfect to 'unpredictable'. They took a bit of looking after – especially as we were also to prepare lunch for everyone and host a BBQ for participants and spouses in the early evening. I'm pretty sure that Andy wasn't expecting to be changing the nappy of someone else's one-year-old at 10.30 in the morning. I was surprised too to find myself shoving a plastic tractor and trailer around the garden with a one-year-old in the back and a stroppy 3-year-old in the driver's seat. The latter, from the house of the sniffing dog, surprised the gathering by attaching himself to mother's nipple during luncheon. Fortunately, the noise from the automated pool cleaner all but drowned out the fearsome slobbering noises. Lunch was saved from complete disaster due to the delicious Foie Gras supplied by one of the fit-clubbers. Not your force-fed stuff, this was organically reared and quite unobjectionable –

to me at least.

On Sunday morning, following that chaos, Jan and I went to a street market at St. Antonin, 10 km distant. It is a lovely town in a valley among the oak forests where the market spreads throughout the town from the main square like spokes on a wheel. It is hugely popular, not least with the British, who probably make up a quarter of the throng. Stalls offer wonderful fayre - cakes, bread, wine, honey, clothes, fruit, veggies and er……onion bhajis and pakoras! We hear Surrey English everywhere but if I'd wanted to go to Surrey, I'd have gone to Surrey. I blame neither the expats nor the stallholder but to me this is not France and despite the beauty of the place, were I to be given a house there, I would sell it and move on.

Now contrast this with our (English) friends who also live nearby. We were invited for lunch and had a jolly time eating chicken (cooked) in their garden. We usually wait to be invited somewhere unlike my brother who often arrives at parties without invitation under the pretext, 'I've just come along to show I'm not offended at not being invited'. Our hosts, Sue and Ulick (what a nice couple they are) have integrated into the town and learned the language. Indeed, Ulick was even asked recently to sit on the town council. He declined citing the nuances of both local politics and lack of technical French as excuses. Plus, the fact that one meeting he was invited to as a 'trial run' didn't finish till well after midnight!

While my wife did a psychic reading I went for a 'mystery tour' passing through the delightfully named village of Les Tourettes and saw a tiny church called Chapelle Notre-Dame des Graces with stunning views over wooded valleys. I actually ended up in the city of Cahors in biblical rain. Boy is this place busy, even in the deluge the only parking spot was in an underground car park, notable for sharing the space with part-dug archaeological ruins of the early Roman town. I did have reasons for visiting a town, I wanted to buy writing paper and I needed stamps to post a letter for Jan. After a few false starts I found a papetterie which sold writing paper. They didn't sell stamps so I had to cross the main road to a tabac to buy them. There wasn't a post box outside the tabac so I had to re-cross the road to post Jan's letter – in the post box next to the writing paper shop! Knackered after all this exercise I'd had enough.

'Fit Club' apart we had a lovely time catching up with our mates and shared a bottle or six over a meal or two before heading off towards Buzet-sur-Baisse and our friends Terry and Sandra. He has a penchant for a drop of the red stuff so Buzet is an appropriately named base. We stayed in a brand-new self-contained studio which is part of a B & B set-up in nearby Damazan. We originally booked for one night but Terry had organised a lunch at a nearby restaurant for our second day there so we extended it to two. Price for one night – 40 Euros. Price for 2 nights – 60 Euros per night! Work that one out. No amount of haggling could raise the price even further so we put a dent in our budget and accepted their terms.

The lunch was at a small restaurant in a tiny village with no other commerce, the kind of place you'd only happen upon by mistake. From the front it looked like one property in a row of terraced houses but it opened up inside to seat perhaps thirty. On arrival we were offered Floc de Gascogne (a local aperitif made from Armagnac and white wine, flavoured with local fruits) or alternatively, chilled white wine (multiple of either if you wanted them). The meal consisted of eggs mimosa for appetiser, Tagliatelle 'bolognaise' with melted cheese for main (an enormous bowl for the six of us that they took away part way through – and bought it back full again) which was really delicious. For desert we had eggy cherry flan followed by cheese and bread. They supplied all the wine we could drink plus a bottle of Armagnac on the table as a settler – and coffee. A fabulous meal, all home cooked, including all the booze – 10 Euros per head! We understand that the local commune 'sponsors' the restaurant in an effort to bring souls to the village. You eat what they offer – no choice, but it was one of the best meals I have ever eaten and Tuesday lunchtime the place was nearly full.

I bought a box of Buzet wine from the local Vignoble outlet (a cooperative that distributes local wines) which was good, if strong at 14 percent. Terry buys his from the same place filling his own 10-litre containers from one of three 'petrol pumps' offering wine between 1.60 and 2.40 euros per litre. His was in the middle at 1.80, a delightful drop of red if a bit dangerous at that price.

The River Baisse was down a metre from its peak due to recent flooding but was still a torrent as we left heading for Pyla, south of The Arcachon Basin. As we drove west, deciduous forest, primarily oak, gave way to regimented pine as we neared the Atlantic coast. Steel-framed fire-watch towers rise periodically above the forest on the look-out in the tinder-dry woodlands. We passed through a delightful village which has arched colonnades / palisades on each side of its main square offering shade from the heat and a playground for the lone inhabitant not having lunch. We stopped the car to soak it up. Apart from the gentle scuffing of the local man's shoes as he ambled past dormant shops in the shade, the silence was total. The harsh, brittle sun scorched honey-coloured flagstones and a motionless dog watched without interest from the shaded steps of the Marie. It was like a scene from a film – a tense, silent pause before a lone rider clip-clops into town before entering the saloon through swinging doors. Except here, it appeared that the place was so sound asleep that nothing would ever happen again.

The Dune de Pyla (or Pilat) is the largest sand dune in Europe rising over 100 metres and extending four kilometres along the Atlantic coast. It is a major attraction which I suppose justifies the 4-euro parking fee, although had we been driving a Mini we may have plunged in to one of the substantial potholes, never to escape. We run the gauntlet of 'tacky Alley', an assortment of cafes, restaurants and souvenir shops squabbling for tourist bucks in the shade of the pines. The dune itself rises straight from the forest and is climbed via a sand-swamped stairway. The soft sand, pale and sun-scorched, affords little purchase as we drag ourselves up with the help of a rope handrail. The views are stunning with the northern coast of the Arcachon Basin scything round to Cap Ferat, due west. The Atlantic Ocean beyond sweeps away over sand bars to the south. Behind us the pine forest stretches inland as far as the eye can see. There are too many people up there for my liking - it's a moment that should be appreciated in isolation - or with just my wife perhaps – if we both keep quiet.

There is a good proportion of Northern Europeans here – Dutch (they are everywhere), Scandinavians and lots of Brits, many of whom have overindulged the lager over the winter and look like hairless, pink porkers in too-brief clothing – looking rather like me in fact. Down below again, we bypass the cafes and share a picnic bench with a friendly family of ants. Presumably there are no picnic tables to encourage people into the restaurants – perhaps they've introduced colonies of ants for the same reason – perhaps ants prefer picnic titbits left on benches to restaurant food.

Our B & B is in Gujan-Mestras, a few kilometres from Pyla, and is run by Danni and Jacques (who is partially recovered from a severe stroke). Jan had a dip in their pool then sat in front of the fire with a muffler on as a hot day gives way to a chill evening. Our room was Chinese-themed throughout, down to the terracotta bed which was appalling. They were nice people though and we shared breakfast with the two other guests, a 50-something man and wife from 'just south of' Paris. They were beautifully attired and probably pretty wealthy but he'd recently been made redundant and wasn't due for retirement for ten years or so. They were sharing our B & B but looked like they should have been somewhere else (The George V in Paris perhaps) – they were friendly and chatty and we gleaned that this was their first 'chambre d'hote tour'. I gathered they were rather enjoying it. Incidentally, Royal suite in the George V is approximately 25,000 euros per night - our Chinese 'womb' in Gujan-Mestras B & B was 53 euros (including substantial breakfast). Irritatingly Danni, our hostess, stood by and chatted throughout breakfast so Jan's timing had to be immaculate when scooping our picnic lunch into her handbag.

We are at the central point of the southern shore of the Arcachon Basin near the Atlantic coast and decide to travel north up the western bank of the Gironde and cross the mouth of the river by car ferry to Royan. I wish the 20-minute crossing had been longer because the day is calm, the sun is out and the view is beautiful. We are heading for St. Georges de Didonne just south of Royan, specifically the camp site of Bois Soleil where we caravanned when I was a child nearly fifty years ago. These days there are a few permanent, air-conditioned chalets where we used to park our van. Long ago, the bays were marked out with a few pinecones – low, manicured hedges now, but that apart there were no substantial changes. It was rougher and readier back in our day but the on-site takeaway where we used to buy buckets of frites has changed in name only. Back then the camp store was a Coop and I remembered my Dad discovering a wine called Rochdale. We are from near Rochdale and, as the Cooperative movement had started there, they named a 'cheeky little number' after it. We re-discovered the camp site on the web in about 5 seconds, but imagine having to organize a trip for 3 kids, 2 adults, a mirror sailing dinghy, a caravan and all attendant paraphernalia without the internet! Actually, it transpires that it is the 50th anniversary of the camp site so they had produced a commemorative brochure with comparative photographs from our era to the present. It was a perfect time for a re-visit – and rather nostalgic.

We stayed in a small hotel in St. Georges-de-Didonne (60 euros, no breakfast but clean) and I walked the four kilometres to Royan along the beach on a perfect summer evening (while Jan prepared the following day's picnic). I've decided that when we finally settle down it will be by the sea – if I can get Jan to agree – if we can afford it.

We now head inland to Oradur sur Glane roughly 200 km away, near Limoges. Oradur is a town that has been left just as it was from 10th July 1944 when 642 inhabitants were slaughtered by the Nazis in an appalling massacre – retaliation apparently for recent partisan activity in the region. Burned out vehicles, agricultural machinery, bicycles and even spinning jennies remain from that awful day amid razed buildings, rusty and frozen in time as a 'living' memorial to the 190 men, 247 women and 205 children who died in the carnage. There are signs on the walls of partially destroyed buildings - butcher, cafe, dentist, 'coiffeur' for example that, up to that dreadful day, tell of a small town living its life as best it could in war-torn France. There are rusty tram-tracks below dead overhead powerlines, manicured lawns and a dimly-lit underground memorial whose display cases house spectacles, watches and other personal effects found among the debris – it's these items, many cracked and twisted, that really personalise the slaughter. Neither Jan nor I heard a bird sing during our visit – and believe me it was quiet enough to hear them.

Accommodation that evening was another chambres d'hote, Le Moulin de Fauvette, run by an English couple, Mike and Amanda who run a great ship. They are chatty and hard-working and our stay was a pleasure. Other guests included a French man desperate to get the internet so he could watch Jo-Wilfried Tsonga lose in the French Tennis Championship and an English couple driving a 1936 MG to a rally, whose conversation was limited to......well, 1936 MGs! We endured a terrific storm in the early evening which flooded our hosts cellar and washed the gravel drive into a heap. Tomorrow's drive home will be a gentle 500-kilometre canter but today belongs to Oradur sur Glane.

Our little trip was two weeks. What a fascinating, diverse country and we barely scratched the surface.

Since our adventure we've parted company with the car – exchanged it for a friend's camper van. We met halfway to do the swap. He drove home at 130 kilometres per hour, I drove home at 80. If I hadn't had to stop four times to fill up with diesel I would have been home a bit sooner – yes, it's a bit thirsty. The car was ten years old; the van is twenty-three. The car was quiet, the van isn't. But we didn't carry a lavatory around in the car. I'll tell you more about the camper in due course.

The present, back on the boat....

Our general direction is north west and we have decided that we haven't time to tackle the Canal de La Somme which was on our original itinerary. Friends have told us it's lovely and we don't want to compromise our enjoyment of it by rushing. So, we have a decided to make our way straight to Belgium. We can take either The St. Quentin Canal or the Canal du Nord. The latter is bigger and faster, the former (allegedly) prettier - but with a notorious tunnel.

We opted for the St. Quentin so head north. The canal is generally pleasant but, in our opinion at least, doesn't begin to compare with the beauty of the Nivernais, Bourgogne or the four canals of the Route Bourbonaise between the rivers Seine and Saone. I'm not sure what it is really. Perhaps it's our relative proximity to busier industrial towns now we are further north. Where the smaller, more southerly canals have a ramshackle charm, here they appear more unkempt and generally grubbier. Maybe they are not as touristy so the lockkeepers and authorities have less incentive to beautify locks and towpaths. It's certainly very quiet, we see very few boats.

St. Quentin port itself was free, including services (electricity and water).

For some reason no-one can be bothered to actually manage the place. Good for us now, but you would imagine it can only go downhill in time. The whole port area is fenced in. Unless you find someone who has the key-code for the single gate, you're stuck. We were given the code by a lady on an Australian-flagged boat who kindly invited Jan to go on board and use their wifi to download a few emails. Sadly, the lady hadn't discussed it with her husband and he overturned his wife's decision. Jan left hurriedly – rather embarrassed. Saint-Quentin is home to Kafétien Gomis, a French Athlete. He is a long jumper and the last person to escape the port without a password when he freed himself by leaping over the canal.

It is an interesting town, the centre of which is perched up on a hill a kilometre or so from the port, and rather a hike. Founded by the Romans it was devastated during the first World War. It was in the heart of the war zone because the Germans integrated it into the Hindenburg Line and as a consequence, it suffered badly. In fact, 80% of its buildings, including the Basilica, were damaged. Despite that, the centre is still very impressive. Despite an intense search, I was unable to find any canal charts that would help us further on.

We did have a treat while there. The Patrouille de France, the French Aerobatic Display Team (equivalent of the UK's Red Arrows) were doing a display close by. We had a privileged view of some marvellous manoeuvres including multi-coloured smoke trails, loops and rolls. Great skills.

This display was of particular interest to me because I had some involvement with the Red Arrows through work in the UK in a fund-raising capacity. They flew into an airfield in Shropshire (Ternhill if I recall correctly) and joined us at a charity golf tournament at Hawkstone Park where proceeds were split between the Red Arrows Trust, their charitable arm, and a cricketer's benevolent fund with which we worked. As a result of this Jan and I were invited to go and see an ISP - an In Season Practice. Every summer the pilots have a break of two or three weeks away from a very busy schedule. Before they resume their displays they do a number of private run-throughs to make sure they are as polished as ever. It was a fascinating day for us. We were invited to join the pre-flight briefing where they decide the sequences they'll perform that day. Then we stood next to the runway with the tenth (reserve) pilot as the jets thundered by. The guy with us had a radio so we could hear the communication between the pilots, particularly 'Red One', the leader, as he called each manoeuvre. For example, he would call 'Smoke on' and trails of coloured smoke would fill the sky. It was a real privilege to witness. Every routine is filmed and at the post-flight briefing the pilots examine everything in detail on a big screen, even to the point of criticizing each other if something wasn't perfect. Skilled pilots they may be but as golfers some of them would make good plumbers!

Riqueval Tunnel

What people really associate with the Saint-Quentin Canal is the tunnel so here is our experience........

After 11 years and many thousands of kilometres living on 3 different boats, I've finally encountered a vessel that makes more noise than us - and is even slower.... namely the beast that pulls convoys through the Riqueval tunnel. The tug is known in French as the Toueur (tower). Because there is no ventilation, engines are forbidden in the tunnel so the tug is electrically powered – a little like the old tram system where an extending arm sucks power from over-head cables. The 5760-metre tunnel is well lit (a fluorescent every 30 metres or so) and there are plenty of blue flashes and showers of sparks from the tug's electrical umbilical. Although this electrical activity is a bit unnerving deep underground, it is silent - the noise comes because the tug is chain-driven. There is a constant din - clackety-clackety-clackety - as the chain, which runs the full length of the tunnel, passes over the cogs on the boat that haul the tug through at about 4 km per hour. The whole chain apparently weighs about 96 tonnes! The racket is a little tortuous, compounded because it echoes in the confined space. The sound changes too because the tunnel walls are alternating brick, rock and render – a harsh echo from brick and rock but slightly dampened by the concrete render. The tunnel height also varies from time to time so the clackety rhythm changes subtly as we creep through.

I had been slightly worried by our impending passage so had sought guidance on what to expect via internet forums and personal chats. I reckoned I'd made all possible preparations. Boats go through in convoy, largest behind the tugboat to the smallest. Sometimes you can ask too many questions – for example we were advised 'for definite' that two crossed ropes were best, in other words from the boat-in-front's starboard stern bollard to our port fore bollard and opposite. Then someone else said that one rope – minimum 30 metres – off-side stern to our off-side fore was the way to go, particularly for larger boats. We're a medium boat. One contributor said that they were currently in discussion with their insurance company over damage sustained during their passage. Another said that they were following the tug when it caught fire. Others said they were going to avoid the tunnel altogether and take the 'safer', but less scenic, Canal du Nord. A week before our passage I knew nothing – the day before, too much.

I measured out three 30 m lengths of rope on the quay in St. Quentin port. One big thick length for a single rope passage and two 30m lengths cobbled together from our usual mooring lines, for a 'crossed-rope' passage. I'd been quite precise too - after a couple of false starts. Initially I measured 30 decent paces but soon realized that this was a bit haphazard so instead measured six lengths of my 5m tape measure along the quay. (Good job I did because, having short legs, 30 of my paces only came out to about 23 metres. I would have needed a series of mini long jumps to get anywhere near the required length). The big, thick, single rope was two joined up bits of really industrial-strength stuff that came with the boat, and I could barely lift it – so I rather hoped for a 2-rope passage.

Then there was fendering. I'd perhaps been over-thinking things having envisioned us in the middle of a convoy. Ok, imagine this - the tugboat at the front holds a straight line because its running over a huge chain and hugging the wooden rubbing-board against the towpath. But the second boat starts to drift to one side and has to correct itself with a turn of its rudder – no engine remember. Because the second boat's rear end is now swinging about, the nose of the third boat begins to swing about even more – see where I'm going with this? I can imagine that we, say 5th boat in the convoy, are in the middle of a writhing snake and being whipped from side to side like a terrier with a rat, crashing from one wall to the other. Yes, I'd need some fendering. We've got 'a bit of an assortment' of fenders, most picked up en route out of the canal - some actually have air in them. These went around the boat in a nasty, uncoordinated lifebelt. I've got four tyres which I roped and installed, one at each corner – these would provide our primary protection.

We arrived at the tunnel at 4.30pm (an hour after the last north-bound convoy had departed) having left St. Quentin at about 1.00pm. This timing was planned as I favoured an early-morning passage. Having said that, there's no indication of passage times posted near the tunnel and I'd long since learned not to trust information on the internet. In fact, the only sign near the tunnel tells you it's a 'Péage' – in other words you pay a toll. What it didn't say was how much and that you couldn't pay cash – they send an invoice to a registered address which you have to provide by means of an official invoice or such-like before you go through.

I was a bit ratty because I'd lost one of my five big mooring spikes. Trying to supplement the badly spaced bollards, I'd decided to put a stake in. The first 4 inches of towpath is soil so tapped the top of the spike till it was free-standing before giving it a proper whelt with the sledgehammer. Annoyingly after 4 inches you strike bedrock. My first real hammer-blow was a teeth-jarring affair. The spike hit rock, leapt in the air and cartwheeled straight into the canal.

We spent the night in the depths of a deep, damp cutting which, although fairly well lit, was a little lonesome - until a journalist arrived. He was Canadian, from Toronto, who was on assignment covering the 1st World War commemorations. He invited himself to come and have a drink with us (persuasive chap he was) – 'I'll just go and fetch my wife', he said, 'she could do with some company'. He was a Forensic Ballistician as well as a journalist and she was a very amusing Mexican lady (Patty) who was somewhat relived to get away from their hire-car. That afternoon husband Ted had dug up a live 77mm shell which was now in the boot of their car.

'Should be fairly safe', he said.

He travelled round with a metal detector and could tell where shell and bullet casings were manufactured and who had used them. He even reckoned to be able to work out what had happened during a particular skirmish by studying the nature and position of discarded munitions. It's not every day you come across a Forensic Ballistician. Actually, it was an interesting distraction from our forthcoming passage, helping me overcome my nerves for a spell.

I awoke at 3.00am.

Four hours and twenty minutes later the 3-man tug crew arrived – looking rather more refreshed than me – thankfully. We are lucky actually because we are the only boat going through. I was so pleased that my little plan seemed to be working (early morning, solo passage) that I ran a 'happy flag' up the mast. Then I was instructed to take the mast down. Is one boat towing another a convoy?

I'd done everything I could think of to prepare for our passage so started our engine and moved up into position behind the tug. Jan stood ready with all our ropes, ready to pass on the appropriate one. Tension was building. Would it be a single or a crossed pair? Neither!! One of the tug men passed us their rope instead! Roughly 30 metres long, it was attached to the left rear of the tug. The rope divided two thirds of the way back to us so we could attach one branch to each of our forward bollards. A few hand-signals (which I presumed were friendly) before I shut down our engine and we were off. We had to round a slight bend before the tunnel proper – which I had also been worried about, fearing us being whipped sideways into the wall – but to start with the speed was minimal and into the tunnel we went without a hitch. Gradually the pace increased in proportion to the noise and we reached cruising speed – about four kilometres per hour or a steady walking pace.

Despite all my angst it was really straightforward passage – dare I say it, rather tedious. I do find that the more preparations you make, the less hassle you encounter. It's when you approach something on a wing and a prayer that you can find trouble - it can creep up and, on occasion, become pretty dangerous – such as leaving Dunkirk - I'll tell you about that later. Throughout the passage we didn't touch the sides once, there was plenty of light and I even managed a cup of coffee. There were markers on the wall every 10 metres counting down to zero (heading north). After what seemed like an age one said 4980. Every now and then there was writing spray-painted on the walls. Either memorials to people who had perished on the passage or idiots leaving their mark, often written in English.

An hour and forty minutes after setting off we were out. The noise largely died as the din from the clackety chain was released skyward then faded away altogether as the tug came to a halt. We started the engine, loosed the lines and away we went.

What it would have been like as part of a convoy I don't know. It is a bit peculiar moving through a tunnel without the engine but, for us at least, it was fine.

BIG Canals

On the St. Quentin canal, Cambrai was a place we'd really looked forward to. One of the best-known ports on the system, we thought to stay for a week while two sets of guests came and stayed. No chance. The port had been emptied because there was a huge Ascension Day firework display and even without the fireworks we were told that the port was full to capacity. Peculiar really, not only because it's pretty much peak cruising season when many boats would be out on trips, but also because a couple of weeks ago we'd seen one boat many miles from home, and I know they moor at Cambrai. They may well have reserved that spot for another visitor but we were made to feel about as welcome as a slug in a salad by the port captain. An English couple tried to help us find somewhere to welcome our guests but a particular Antipodean crew were 'aloof' (to be polite). Perhaps they were just embarrassed because they'd made a hash of extricating themselves from St. Quentin port a couple of days earlier. Previous to that they'd been hauled through the Riqueval tunnel but left their engine running – unfortunately they were spotted because theirs is a boat that smokes a lot. The smarter the boat, the more noticeable the cock-ups.

We find instances like ours at Cambrai very few and far between but I can only relate what happens to us.

Compare the above with the wonderful experience in the Gare D'Eau at Courcelles lés Lens where, to be frank, we had a bit of a result. We've struggled to find decent moorings over the past couple of weeks, often mooring above or below locks. This is particularly true on the Grand Gabarit. The previous night for example we were right next to big double locks in the centre of

Douai - certainly not for the faint-hearted! Admittedly it's largely down to me because we are lacking decent charts. We'd been told we could buy the real thing in a specialist shop in Douai. I cycled into town, got hopelessly lost and got tangled up with a major road-improvement scheme - and when I got there the shop had closed down! The lock mooring we ended up on was relatively secure on two key-side bollards. In addition, we had a rope lashed round some old iron framework with a succession of revolting knots. Seriously big boats came through the locks regularly – pretty close to us too. The two locks are 144 metres and 90 metres long respectively. About 14 million litres of water between the two. The flooding of the locks sloshes water about up and down the canal and the water level drops about a foot each time. Our dear old boat bounced about and swung to and fro on her mooring. Luckily the locks stopped working at 9.00 pm and didn't start till a civilized 06.30 the following morning - so we had time for some kip. I'd read somewhere that there was electricity available too. Well, the only supply I could find was powering a pizza restaurant a couple of hundred metres away. Actually, I'd messed that up too – the electricity was on another mooring nearby.

There is a port off the main canal, which apparently would have been fine for a barge our size. The problem is that it was beyond where we moored and, if we'd gone down the lock and found it unsuitable, we would have had to move on, and it was getting a bit late in the day. Overall, just poor planning.

Before Douai we stayed in the Bassin Rond at the junction of the St. Quentin and the Canal de Sensée (part of the Grand Gabarit). This is a big lake, off the main waterway, which had presumably been a major commercial hub in years gone by. Now it is home to a few 40-metre péniches and a couple of dozen cruisers in various states of decay. But we had a pleasant and safe mooring on a small floating pontoon down a little inlet – even if it did rain all night and the slime on the pontoon made it like an ice rink.

On to Courcelles. The mooring is basically in a sizeable lake accessed via a short channel off the main commercial canal. It wasn't easy to tell from information and photographs on the internet but it appeared that there was also a little inner port off the main lake, or Gare d'Eau as it was labelled. When we arrived the little port was indeed tiny and too small for us, but we moored in the main lake on small group of floating pontoons.

Now, finally, a bit of decent planning! I'd phoned the Marie at Coucelles from Douai the previous day because it said on the web that the municipality had taken over the running (or responsibility for) the port. Actually, as far as I can see that means doing bugger all. My phone call yesterday was probably the first actual mooring enquiry they'd had this year. It had obviously caught them unaware and I was asked to 'wait a moment' a few times before I was connected to someone who actually knew they had a port. Thereafter the cogs of local bureaucracy ground faultlessly. They were very friendly and shouldered the responsibility saying that we could come and moor - for free - and to ring the Marie on arrival if we wanted electricity. Splendid.

So, we arrived and moored – after a couple of false starts. Firstly, on a sloping bank that was too shallow and another on the hammerhead of a pontoon that, we were told by Cedric, a boating resident, was broken. We finally moored up (on Cedric's advice) next to another boat the same length as us with a big 'No Mooring' sticker in the window.

'You'll be fine there', he told us, 'that sticker is for small boats only'.

There are plenty of electric points so I went to try and plug into one. Cedric, now joined by his mate, rushed over and said that there were only 5 power-points working in the port, out of a possible thirty – and they were all being used, full time, by the five residents here! I was rather tetchy from our previous struggles on the Grand Gabarit. 'What is it with this bloody canal?' I asked them. Then I calmed down a bit and phoned the Marie who said they'd send someone to help.

A short time later a man of some bulk with a determined look on his face arrived with his pretty young assistant (female). They really had no idea of the workings of their port and certainly weren't aware that all the functioning electricity points were taken, so I explained the problem.

'Oh', they said.

There's an adjacent log cabin, that used to be the responsibility of the 'Capitaine du Port' before his role was taken over by the municipality, so I suggested that I could plug into a socket in there and run a lead to the boat – which they thought was a brilliant idea! They both looked impressed with my thinking – in fact had the municipal budget extended, they'd have probably offered me a position there and then as port facilitator. They made a few phone calls and eventually they managed to get hold of the guy who has the key to the cabin. Turns out that this is the guy who was the port captain before he was fired - and he lived about 100 metres away! He mooched up, looking a little disgruntled and unlocked the cabin. Then four Gendarmes arrived – not on official duty, though dressed for it, they were just out for a stroll apparently. They stopped for a chat – handshakes and smiles all round.

So, standing around debating the electrical difficulties of a fat Englishman were: two municipal representatives, one former port captain and current log-cabin key-holder, two blokes who told me there was no electricity available, four Gendarmes and me. Then the chap whose boat we are moored up against arrived to find a 'gathering' outside his boat. He's called Hubert, and he, Cedric and I are all getting on rather well together.

The gendarmes had moved on but I offered the remainder of the party a glass of wine to say thank you for going the extra metre for us.

'No, no, no thank you,' the boss from the Marie said, flapping his hand with a dismissive motion. 'That's very kind but no, thank you all the same. No, we must return to work. We have much to do. We are extremely busy today. Thank you, but no, no............oh, OK then, just a small one'.

I went to get my wine and electricity leads and hey presto – through a window, over the patio, across a path, down a bank, across the pontoon, across my neighbours' boat - we have power!

It's all 'on the municipality' we were told, so no charge. So, we're staying till Monday! Actually, that's Wednesday now as I've had to order a new top to my water strainer for the generator which has cracked, and the replacement won't get here till Tuesday via Poste Restante in nearby Courcelles Lés Lens. You don't really want to be stuck on any canal with a leak, particularly not one this busy.

Hubert, our temporary neighbour, was a decent chap but was not used to having a boat moored next to him. This manifested itself when Jan returned from a short dog walk to find three mouldy tomatoes on our side-deck. Hubert had lobbed them out of his kitchen window forgetting he had company. We had a good chuckle when I thanked him for his gift.

But we were made really welcome, we're in a safe haven off a big highway and it's a great place to have guests. But, as Jan pointed out yesterday, it's doing things a little out of your comfort zone that gives you a buzz and lets you know you're alive – I mean travelling on the big waterways, not being pelted by rotten fruit.

Forty metres away across the picnic area, down a bank, is a dog-training school. A fairly substantial one too. There are groups of people doing general obedience classes but also advanced groups teaching collies and the like to run through tunnels and do slaloms etc. As the old joke goes, if you're being chased by a police dog, don't run through a tunnel or jump through a hoop, they're trained for that!

Last night they were training till 11.15 in the evening. Dogs and trainers yapped noisily under floodlights, dive-bombed by clouds of insects. The reason for this late-night session is now obvious, they have a competition tomorrow. The whole arena had been laid out with assault-courses, judging marquees and spectator areas. Should be a quiet, peaceful Sunday.

Courcelles is a real mix of a place. I found three supermarkets. A scruffy Intermarché supermarket, a new and pristine Leclerc superstore and a Halal supermarket whose name I don't know as I don't speak Arabic (or whatever it was). But it was certainly a friendly town, particularly the municipal delegation and the staff in the post office who helped with my package. It's about 100 kilometres from Calais and right on the motorway system which is possibly why there is such a 'diverse' population.

Our mate John came and went, having delivered a few tins of paint that would keep me out of mischief for a few hours. He's on his way back to St. Jean de Losne where he has a lovely house and is someone else we will see little of in the future. We'll miss him, not only because he's a good friend, but also he loves our dog, Tache, who used to go and visit 'uncle' John regularly and charge around the garden. My sister and brother-in-law came and went with their smart bicycles and super-fit legs. It was (almost) like being on a care-free mooring on one of the smaller central canals – except here we had the threat of having to join the big canals again when we left.

Dunkirk and on to Belgium

The Canal Dunkerque-Escaut is a 189 km long and is a series of large canals stretching south-east from Dunkirk to Montagne-du-Nord. As far as I could make out, the route is also known as The Liaison, La Liaison au Grand Gabarit, Canal au Grand Gabarit, Dunkerque-Escaut Waterway and Liaison Dunkerque-Escaut. Whatever you call it, it's a big waterway, industrial and not over-clean in places. Grand Gabarit is not 'big rubbish', no, Gabarit refers to the dimension of boats on here, as in 'big gauge'. And some of them are big. This is a highway geared up for commercial boats – a big thoroughfare to be endured rather than savoured. We joined it after an extension of the St. Quentin Canal, with roughly 150 kilometres to travel from there to Dunkirk.

There are limited overnight stopping places and you need to get off the main waterway because commercial boats up to 120 metres in length thunder by regularly. Laden ones, which can weigh a couple of thousand tonnes, going about 9 kph and empty ones doing 15 kph both rock you about a bit as they pass but moored on the concrete banks it would be very uncomfortable, if not outright dangerous.

We've been spoilt really. Having been based in St. Jean de Losne we had some fabulous waterways within striking distance. Safe, small canals that are somehow represent the impression we always had of an archetypal French waterway. As you're helped along by friendly, and largely very efficient, VNF employees you really can find yourself in another world. You pass timeless villages that really haven't changed much in a hundred years. Great to see but, because they haven't moved on, many are slowly dying and some nowadays don't even have a bakery. Between settlements, huge expanses of open country with farmland, forest and endless skies.

As we get further north it just seems busier and rather more frantic.

As described, Courcelles was a lovely surprise, Bethune was a surprise of a different nature. There is one 20 metre pontoon found 700 metres down an arm off the main waterway. When we got there at 12-metre cruiser was on the mooring. Owned by an English guy, Tom, with his mate Raymond, who were very accommodating and moved up enough so we could perch on the end with nearly half our boat overhanging. But at least we had somewhere to stay the night. The town (defended largely by British forces) was largely undamaged during the war so still retains some fabulous architecture, mainly centred round a large, paved square. It's about a kilometre from our pontoon but the canal used to run right to the town centre before it was filled in and houses built on the reclaimed ground – a great shame for boaters but convenient for those who now live there.

Because we cruise with our mast down I've had to adapt the forward navigation light which we needed from time to time because of early-morning autumn mist. The mist is patchy and even though you may set off in sunlight, the mist can develop a little later. Because you can't stop, you need lights. Some of the bigger boats have radar but not all and because we are under 20-metres long, thereby classed as a 'small craft', we have no official standing on the waterways and just have to keep out of everyone's way.

Leaving Bethune at 9.00am it was a perfect sunny morning. We'd just got back on the main waterway when the fog came from above and the duckweed came from below, and things generally turned a bit nasty. The mist soon cleared but the weed was a big problem for us. It would continue to be so till we passed the junction of the River Lys after a couple of hours. It's here you can turn north up the river towards Ghent. The weed got thicker and thicker and the engine threatened to over-heat twice as our filters got clogged up. We couldn't moor on the side so the only way to sort things out was to wait for a big gap in the traffic and stop the engine midstream. Jan steered (our big rudder enables us to steer even at 1 kph) while I cleared the filter as the boat drifted slowly along. It's not very pleasant and you just pray that the engine restarts – which it does thankfully, both times. It was like driving through pea soup as the big boats churned the water into a seething green broth. After the Lys it all cleared up and it became less unpleasant as we headed for the 13-metre-deep lock near Arques.

On approach there is rather a wait till the big lock fills up and by the time the gates open an empty 80-metre barge has arrived and goes in before us. The lock is 144-metres long but has gates about 2/3rds of the way down to shorten the lock if necessary (thereby using less water I presume). There is barely room for the two of us and we've just tied on to the floating bollards, set into the walls, when the lock begins to empty. We are only a metre behind the rear of the commercial boat and its back end looms over our bow. As the water-level drops, the cill appears at the back of the lock and it's only two feet from the back of our rudder. It is a very tight squeeze and the skipper on the rear rope is rather alarmed. The problem is that if your rudder gets stuck on the cill at the rear, the front of the boat keeps going down and you can sink nose down in the lock. It's too close for comfort to be honest and we have the collywobbles a bit. If you have plenty of room around you in a lock this deep, there really isn't a problem, but things were very tight. It got rather claustrophobic the further down the forty or so feet we had to drop. Another problem is that when the lock has emptied and the front gates open, water is pushed back into the lock and the boats get flushed backwards a few feet. We only had a metre so there is very little room between us and the one in front. Luckily the skipper of the commercial boat realized this and puts an extra rope on his boat to make sure he doesn't creep back into us when the lock gates opened. We feel very confined and we're mighty glad to get back into the daylight.

Our lock companion has powered away towards a four-metre lock about a kilometre further on, but we decide to stop for the night on a small disused canal on the left (port for those lacking boating knowledge, like me). What we don't really realize is that the water from the big lock above flows in and out of this off-shoot as a sort of 'escape-road' at about five kilometres an hour! The water from the big lock needs an escape route to prevent the next lock being swamped when water pours down the waterway. So, we endure another night of being sloshed about and have to time our departure the following day to avoid the rushing tide!

Next morning we extricate ourselves ('a dumb place to stop' – according to the skipper) and set off - next stop Dunkirk. It turns out to be another long and difficult day. We're pass numerous commercial boats coming the other way and are also overtaken by a few. These included a big pusher-tug shoving a big 'caison' (floating bucket), which according to the sign on its flank, 'carries the equivalent of 80 road trucks'. These beasts do creep up on you from behind with a monstrous inevitability. Sometimes you just want to drive into a lay-by until they get past, but there aren't any. Actually, we were fine, it's just the size of the damn things and the growl of the engines as they pass that makes us realize how vulnerable we actually are.

Near Watten the canal forks. To the left is the route to Calais, but we go right on the Bourbourg canal towards 'Dunkirk Old Port'. Sounds nice eh? Mmmm……we encounter some of the most unpleasant smells we've ever come across – and that includes my BBQs. A variety of odours, chemical, electrical and general industrial make us feel quite dizzy. We're not far from Dunkirk and amidst heavy industry. I suppose this is where the real work of the commercial barges goes on. The canal ends at a lock that takes you down into the port area and eau salée (brackish water) - but the lights are on double red (shut for lunch!). The lock also has an intermediate set of gates halfway along and only the top half (our half) is full. The lower part which is exposed to the port is choked with weed, wood and rubbish has been blown in by the stiff wind – it's so bad that you can barely see the water.

In the event that the lock is unattended there are a number of ways to alert the authorities. I'd phoned both phone numbers on an adjacent board and called on the VHF radio as requested but got no reply from any of them. At about 5.00 pm we'd just settled down for the evening when the lock-operator came back from lunch and the lights went to red / green (be prepared to move imminently as it's nearly dinner time) and we went down the lock. When the lock gates opened we were faced with a veritable dune of filth – wood, cardboard, paper, bottles all piled up in the lower lock chamber before us. So, I revved hard till we reached all the muck then turned the engine off and ploughed through till we hit clear water when I restarted the motor.

We turned sharp right towards the Dunkirk – Nieuwpoort Canal which begins at a lock 1 km distant.

There are off-shoots and side channels here and there and the route wasn't very clear - we had no proper maps so were relying on our GPS chart-plotter and it all got a bit confusing. Frankly my planning has been appalling – to be polite. It's not surprising we got in a muddle. To help us navigate this particular warren, and places to safely moor, we were using our chart plotter, a road map and a cycling route map obtained from a tourist information office! We were about to get our comeuppance.

The passage through which we are passing is narrow and twisty with high brick-lined walls. The route looks old and grubby and is doubtless little changed since the canal was constructed. The lock we are aiming for rises less than a metre up onto the Dunkirk – Nieuwpoort canal and is set in operation by breaking a 'magic eye' beam. This is sited roughly 50 metres short of the lock under a road bridge. Immediately after this bridge another waterway runs across us at right angles. We'd broken the beam but the lights on the lock remained on double red. Our initial objective is lock entrance but as we creep forward, waiting for the lights to tell us the lock is setting (red / green), we notice that there is quite a current flowing with us. Then we see that the flow of water turns to the left immediately after the bridge under which we are waiting. It is only as we emerge we see the water disappearing through a set of sluice gates 25-metres away to the left. As we're creeping forward in the current the lock is still not ready. However, the flow is so strong that we can't stop - and we are being pulled around the corner towards the sluices.

Now this is pretty alarming. The only way out of this pickle is to power across towards the lock entrance, which is basically shaped like a funnel, narrowing down to a point at the lock itself. As we cross we are being pulled to the left by the current and are only a couple of feet from crunching sideways into the high wall on the left as we enter the lock entrance – much too fast – and have to engage full reverse to prevent us colliding with the wall next to the lock. We were very close to getting sucked into the sluices so both of us are a bit 'agitated' as the lock finally opens and we scramble in. Had we had less experience or a less powerful engine we could have been in real bother. Had we had proper charts with detailed information, we wouldn't have navigated this stretch until it was safe to do so.

I believe what happens is that at low tide sluices along the coast are opened to release water from the port / inland areas fed by canal and rivers. It was just bad timing from our point of view but there were no warning signs of any sort.

We are very relieved to ascend the lock but find there is nowhere to stop on the canal because it's basically a narrow, gloomy channel with rocky shores. The first place to pull in is immediately before the first lift-bridge nine kilometres away - which we did – knackered.

The bridge operator arrived to let us through and at 10.00am on Saturday 7th September we left France after five years and entered Flanders.

New Horizons

Part Two

Belgium

'Welcom in Vlanderen' the sign says – welcome to Flanders. The first thing we notice is that the canal is suddenly much tidier with low, concrete banks and a view over the flat countryside. The second thing that strikes us is the avenue of tobacco shops in the first Belgian town we come across, called De Panne. There are around 15 of them spread over a kilometre or so and every third car is English as the Brits make the short trip here from Dunkirk or Calais to stock up 'for their own personal use'. To cash in the Flemish folk also sell booze and chocolate. There's even a Coronation Street tobacco shop!

We arrive in Veurne where we don't get stuck at a lock. We get stuck at a bridge instead. The canal employees have multiple duties, operating lift-bridges and a lock within the town. They also follow boats down the Dunkirk - Nieuwpoort and Lo Canals to open isolated lift bridges on those small rural waterways. This is obviously where the bridge operator was when we pulled up. So, we leave another message on another couple of telephones and settle down for the evening. We're perfectly safe but we have to scrabble up a concrete bank and duck under some railings to get off the boat.

There are cameras at bridges and locks and I'm sure they wait till you've just nodded off before they ring the bell that precedes closing the road to traffic and the lifting of the bridge so we can pass. We're only going 100-metres so we can moor on some proper pontoons for the night and get the dog off.

Moored just round the corner from us is Walter Decock, President of the 'Yacht Club' in Diksmuide where we will be wintering. We've met Walter and his wife Nicky a couple of times while cruising in France. They are a chatty, knowledgeable couple and it was pure fluke that he turned out to be the main man at the very place we applied for a winter mooring.

Diksmuide is one long or five slow cruising days away — we'll take five, down the Lo Canal before joining the small Ijzer River. The Lo canal is tiny, barely bigger than a fat ditch and it's hard to believe we were battling huge boats on the Grand Gabarit a couple of days previously. We are accompanied by the bridge man so presumably someone else is stuck in Veurne till he's finished with us. Before the Lo Canal we traverse the control lock in the centre of town. This is where we are to be officially registered into Belgian waters. The lock keeper checks out our paperwork (license to drive, insurance, etc.) and takes our 80 Euros for six-month cruising license.

At the junction of river and canal is the hamlet of Fintele (pronounced Finteller). We drop onto the river through one of the oldest locks in Belgium, dating from the 1790's. It's a fascinating slice of history, obviously very ancient but well-maintained and operated by an efficient, polite lockkeeper.

Fintele has a population of 30 and is a very pretty, cobbled-street haven with one of the busiest restaurants you'll see anywhere - specialising in eel dishes (paling in Dutch / Flemish, pronounced parling). We stay on the mooring immediately after the lock for three days - replacing some of the paint we'd scraped off en route.

According to Walter this is one of the best moorings in the whole of Belgium. It's free to moor, which apparently is very rare, and if you want electricity it's 3 Euros per day. It is pleasant, in the shadow of the restaurant on the near side and views over farmland on the other. It is also a spot where boats from Nieuwpoort, Diksmuide, Ypres and Veurne come to chill out for a day or two. One skipper seemed a bit agitated that a foreigner on a 19-metre barge was taking up a third of his 'private' mooring. Most people are very friendly though, one walker came down on the pontoon and chatted for an hour or so — in English thankfully, as my Flemish is scratchy! Like Dutch it has too many consonants and employs guttural, throaty noises and there is a danger of an amateur spitting at someone – Phlegmish is perhaps more accurate!

To give you a point of reference we are about 25 kilometres inland from Nieuwpoort on the North Sea coast. About six kilometres in that direction is the off-shoot canal to Ypres (called Ieper here), which is a further 15 km or so from the junction. The river is tiny at this point, in some places barely wide enough for boats to pass. After the Ypres canal junction the river widens as we do the final few kilometres to our destination, Diksmuide (pronounced Diksmurder by some or Diksmyder by others).

This is the terminus of another great trip and we're looking forward to discovering the town and environ. We will be guests of the yacht club, De Ijzervaarders (Iron Sailors). Their port runs linearly for about a kilometre on the edge of town. Near the centre of the port, where their office / clubhouse is located, there is a larger quay where visiting boats can tie. A pleasure trip boat also visits here daily during the season and as we approach it is just tying up at the quay. We are to be 'welcomed' by one of the harbourmasters who will direct us to our mooring. I stop dead in the water to allow the trip boat to finish mooring because it's pretty narrow here, right under the main Diksmuide / Nieuwpoort road bridge that spans the river. Then a shout goes up from a white-haired, white-bearded gentleman who looks a bit like Captain Birds Eye.

'Didn't you see the trip boat?' he yelled.

I'm a bit nonplussed. The reason I have stopped is because I have seen it. It's not easy to miss, it's 40 metres long and a double-decker! To this day I don't know what he was agitated about. He begrudgingly shows us to our temporary mooring by the pump-out machine then demanded 300 Euros for a month's mooring – in cash. I'd arranged a different figure with President Walter so the official had to go and liaise with his boss. This put him in an even fouler frame of mind. He came back again to collect the fee (after we'd cycled into town to draw it out of the bank) and he gave us a rollicking about our Belgian license sticker being in the wrong place. He had to have the final word – so I let him.

It turns out he's an English chap who doesn't like barges and presumably, by extension, bargees. Whether he's got a chip on his shoulder I don't know but I've subsequently talked to a few people who have had the same treatment.

Perhaps you can imagine it. We'd been excited and really looking forward to the next chapter in our little lives only to arrive and have someone spray Round-Up on your begonias. Why did the port choose someone like this to be its public face? Goodness knows.

I must point out that this is the only negative we have experienced here – everybody else has been welcoming, friendly and helpful. The port is clean, secure and well-serviced and the local boaters and officials are fiercely proud of it.

First Look at our New Home

Initial impressions

Belgium doesn't get a good press. Not that it gets a particularly bad press, it just doesn't get much at all. It's often overshadowed by its neighbours - France in particular and to a lesser extent Holland and Germany. Diksmuide, where we're living, is a town in West Flanders – more precisely we're on the outskirts, on a boat on the River Ijzer. From our brief time here and some research I would like to counter a few of the disparaging remarks I have heard. 'Name five famous Belgians', for example. It's not fair. I would like to introduce you to a diverse (some say confused) nation and suggest a few things that make Belgium worthy of better recognition. Its diversity is partly why it has so much to offer. The following is largely a personal endorsement rather than a tourist guide - so first a little about the country....

Belgium is a federal state divided into three regions, The Brussels-Capital region and Flanders in the north and Wallonia in the south - although in eastern Wallonia, within the province of Liege, there is also a small German-speaking region. Basically, French is spoken in Brussels and Wallonia and Dutch in Flanders (or Flemish or Belgian Dutch to be more precise). Each region's culture is influenced by the origins of its people. The political divides are far more complicated. There are numerous political parties basically split into linguistic groups but they all seem to pull in different directions so without coalitions, no single one ever has a chance of ruling. In other words there are no parties that represent Belgium as a whole. Some were created as one-issue parties championing specific cultural, political or economic interests. If you visit for a week you'll be confused. If you visit for 20 years you'll be even more confused. Local people I have spoken to barely understand the complexities so I have no chance. For sanity's sake it's best not to delve too deeply - as long as the trains run and the chip-shop (frituur) is open when required, we're happy. Election time in the U.S. (two parties) or the UK (two plus one plus odds and ends) is bad enough but what it's like here goodness only knows.

Despite this political maze, in our corner of Flanders at least, things appear to run smoothly. Here in Diksmuide the shops are busy, the people are friendly, it's spotlessly clean and, so far, we've felt very safe. We've had some amusing shopping experiences complicated by our struggles with the language (and sign language). My wife's efforts to identify a particular meat in a freezer cabinet had a crowd of fraught Christmas shoppers in fits of laughter. My efforts to buy and replace a car headlamp at a rather smart local car dealership was a near-shambles. Jan was shown kindness and consideration while on a Christmas (window) shopping venture into Diksmuide where the shops in and around the market square bustled with trade and festive spirit. She repaid this benevolence by inadvertently 'stealing' a clothes rail full of rather smart items as she rode away on her cycle. She somehow gets herself into extraordinary situations, on one occasion found herself doing the cha-cha with a complete stranger in a budget supermarket. I'll relate these mishaps in more detail later. At first Belgians appear a serious, furrow-browed race but if you crack the shell there is often a chortle within.

So, what about the lack of 'famous Belgians'? Well, there are plenty - in addition to Eddy Merckx (who is a cyclist by the way, considered by some to be the greatest ever). Born here are Adolphe Sax, inventor of the saxophone, Hergé (the pen name of Georges Remi) who invented Tin Tin, sports stars, Kim Klijsters (tennis) and Jacky Ickx (motor-racing). Baroque painter Peter Paul Rubens is another - so that's enough mickey-taking, that's six to start with – and there is a long list.

Like Diksmuide, nearby Veurne, Ypres and Nieuwpoort appear in similar rude health. Their town centres focus on cobbled market squares that host thriving markets, often overlooked by some imposing and fascinating architecture. Some buildings are original but others were re-built to replicate those shattered during the wars, often paid for with money from German reparations.

Nieuwpoort is on the coast and where inland waterways meet the sea. Because the region is low-lying, particularly areas re-claimed from the sea (known as polders) it's fascinating to see the way the authorities manage the water. At Ganzepoot (Nieuwpoort) six inland waterways flow into the North Sea. Sluices are opened at low tide to release excess water from the rivers, canals and drainage channels, literally draining the land. To witness the egress of water in times of flood is impressive indeed, particularly the eight sluice gates that release water from the River Ijzer.

In October 1914 sluices were opened at HIGH tide and a large area was purposefully flooded – a decisive action that helped bring an end to the Battle of the Ijzer. More about this later.

The region is currently commemorating the 100-year anniversary of the start of the Great War on July 14th, 1914. Visitors from around the world come to see where blood was shed in huge quantities and pay their respects at the many memorials to the brave souls who fought and died here. One such event in October 2014 was a 'Light Show' where 8,500 torchbearers lined the route of an 85-kilometre front which had been established 100 years earlier between Nieuwpoort and Ploegsteert near the French border.

Since our arrival here we've experienced a number of curious coincidences. Most astonishing was when my wife discovered that her uncle, Percy Kershaw, had fought and was severely wounded within a few metres of where we now moor our boat. I'll tell you more about this later as I will about visits to the Menen gate and other nearby memorials.

Diksmuide is well-known for its butter, Belgium as a whole for beer and chocolate. There is ample opportunity to increase your girth but also some very fine food in general. A local lady we spoke to recently told us that French cuisine has its origins here. Maybe, but there is evidence that, despite the name 'French Fries', the chipped potato was eaten in Belgium as early as the 17th Century. You can get these from Frituurs (literally fry-huts). Fish is popular, in particular eel (paling). A favourite is Paling in 't groen (eel in green sauce). Not having tried it I trust it tastes better than it sounds.

A la carte prices are rather rich for our budget with main courses often thirty-plus euros but we've recently found out that restaurants do lunchtime specials, the table d'hote equivalent of France, where a three-course lunch can cost around 12 Euros. That's more within our compass but you get a hearty meal. We went to such an establishment on our wedding anniversary and shared a table with an elderly Belgian couple. We don't speak Dutch; they didn't speak English (which is unusual) so we conversed in French. They extolled the virtues of endives (chicory) wrapped in bacon as one of their local favourites and we tried to explain the delights of Yorkshire Pudding - which was rather testing in a third language. We've previously sampled Europe's hardest biscuit, the couque, which originates from Dinant on the river Meuse. Waffles are popular too, as are speculoos, cinnamon biscuits.

Beer is big. Where others match a wine to a particular dish, some of the Belgians do the same with beer. It's complicated but for example, wheat beers for fish dishes, Blonde beer for eel or chicken, Dubbel for dark meats and fruit Lambic beers to accompany deserts. Figures for how many people have died trying to match the right beer with the right dish are unavailable, but they would doubtless have passed away sated and happy – if they could remember it.

Belgian chocolate (chocolade) is famous world-wide. Indeed, sampling the infinite variety probably would make the world wide. Some of the shop displays are truly wonderful with tray after tray of magnificent, hand-made treats destined straight for the waistline. Manufacture is regulated to maintain quality – a minimum 35% cocoa for example and the requirement to use high-grade fats. I've read that over 2000 chocolate makers (chocolatiers) produce in excess of 172,000 tonnes of 'the food of champions' each year. That's nearly as heavy as me.

There are some magnificent cities in Belgium – major tourist draws. Brussels, Antwerp, Charleroi, Ghent, Liege and Bruges for example are all home to an incredible diversity of architecture, cuisine and culture. As tourist spots these are so well documented generally, I won't elaborate here save to say that driving to and around these places is fraught so you're perhaps better taking the train.

There are 1,500 kilometres of inland waterways in Belgium, canals and rivers. You can travel throughout the country and navigate to the very heart of major cities and see smaller towns and villages. A cruise on the River Meuse in the south-east is a truly wonderful experience through Liege and Namur. You can take trip boats from various locations or rent a hire boat for a week or longer.

One thing that surprised me was how pleasant the coastline is. Huge expanses of clean beaches and sand dunes interspersed with interesting seaside towns. OK, you have holiday apartments but behind these there are lovely town centres. De Haan for example is a wonderful place.

In the UK and France, come the evening, households retreat within as doors, shutters and curtains are closed tight. In a way it's natural to shut out the winter weather and prying eyes. Near us here there are some rather smart apartments which have balconies and huge plate glass windows. By day they have endless views over the flat landscape. If they have curtains or blinds they don't use them, anyone can just peer in – anyone that's impolite that is – like us. For example, one apartment block nearby has ten apartments which, by night, are lit up like a bank of super-size television screens – like mission control during a space mission. They are proud to show off subtle lighting, pot plants and stylish interior décor. They are allowing us into their lounges I hasten to add, not boudoirs or bathrooms, but these ordinary folk appear quite unabashed about allowing us to watch them stage their plays.

So, there's just a taste of Belgium. In conclusion the country has lots to offer. If you like food, cycling, friendly folk or beer you'll find something to suit. Don't listen to the merchants of doom, come and have a look. (I got stuck at six famous Belgians).

Diksmuide

So, we prepare for our first experiences of a new port in a new town in a new country. We're buoyed because the only person we've met who we don't like has gone south for the winter – flown off like a hairy swallow. We'll be sharing the mooring with other over-winterers, Alison and Roger on their Czech-built barge, Iron Maiden.

The whole port is divided into three 'harbours' stretching along the river for over a kilometre. We'll be in harbour 2 – the one where all the important people moor during the season. That's not us, rather club officials and dignitaries – it's like the Directors car park. We have to wait for our final resting place till a couple of dozen cruisers are craned out of the water in the second week in October to overwinter in a nearby shed. Till then we are temporarily rather too close to the pump-out machine for comfort.

We actually arrived a month early, the beginning of September, so the weather is still warm and we get chance to see the town and area still buzzing with tourists. We are in the heart of Flanders and because 2014 is the centenary of the start of the great war, many visitors come to pay their respects on this most awful anniversary.

Their primary focus in Diksmuide is the Ijzertoren (Ijzer Tower) which is a 22-storey tower built by the Flemish people to commemorate their role in the war. It's rather a stark structure with nationalistic and religious overtones and if I were going to use that many bricks I would have built something gentler on the eye. The top section is the shape of a huge, stubby cross with a Flemish flag perched right on top. The letters A.V.V. and V.V.K., also arranged in the shape of a cross, are seen on the eastern and western faces. The letters represent, 'All For Flanders', 'Flanders For Christ'. In large letters around the base of the tower, in three languages, is written 'No More War'. As you approach you pass through the Peace Arch and by the remains of the original tower blown up in 1946. After the war some Flemish people were accused of being collaborators with the Germans and although the bombers were never caught, there is continued speculation that they acted with the approval (or even assistance) of the Belgian state.

Within the tower is a museum arranged floor by floor. You take a lift to get close to the top. From there you can either walk up the remaining couple of floors to the outside viewing platform or begin the descent down seemingly endless stairs to view different scenes and artefacts on the floors below. The view from the top is restricted only by your eyesight or the weather. Because the landscape is snooker-table flat the vista is endless – unless the mist rolls in, which it did for us. There is only a chest-high wall between you and a very long drop – no fencing or ironmongery of any sort, so peering over the edge is rather vertigo-inducing for a chap who prefers to live in a bungalow.

The award-winning museum impressed me, but Jan and our friends Al and Ju were less enamoured, feeling that it didn't depict the misery and suffering sufficiently. Personally, when we finally emerged into the sunlight (the mist has rolled on to annoy someone else), I'd had my fill of misery.

The River Ijzer was an important strategic landmark and reminders of the war are everywhere. A kilometre or so down river is the 'Trench of Death', a refurbished reminder of what misery the soldiers had to endure. They are a fair representation of the make-up of trenches during the war and were occupied by Belgian troops for more than four years during the Battle of the Ijzer. German troops attacked regularly, sometimes within 100 yards so, if you were stationed there you were in constant danger – hence the name, the 'Trench of Death'.

So, what do you do in a strange town? Shopping of course is one necessity. Many people cycle here and the roads and byways are geared up for the cyclist. The town centre is less than a kilometre from the mooring and it's well-endowed with shops, most of which appear to be thriving. No charity shops or 'cash converters', just a good variety of food, clothes and speciality shops. Then on the periphery, supermarkets, DIY warehouses and industry. Our nearest supermarket is only about 300 metres away – one of those German ones with a yellow sign. And, unlike our experience of them in the UK ten years ago, their veggies are of premium quality. It's great that your potatoes haven't gone black before you get off the car park – and there is a butcher in-store too. In the town centre there is a French Carrefour, a little further out a Colruyt, a 'stack 'em high, sell 'em cheap' supermarket which doesn't take cards, it's cash only and we, as I am sure have others, have stood at the till unable to pay. A couple of kilometres in the opposite direction, towards Nieuwpoort, Del Haize, one of a Belgian supermarket chain, the like of UK's Tesco. There are two huge DIY stores to supply everything for the likes of me to make a hash of a project.

Property is not cheap, not London prices but certainly akin to those in other large cities, and it's all very clean and tidy. Apart from the main road through the town, the rest is basically cobbled. It gives the place a certain charm but can give cycling buttocks a painful workout. Could I be described as a cycling buttock – yes, possibly.

Because our mooring is right on the end of harbour 2's pontoon, just after the entrance to a small service canal, and past a bend, we are actually perched out away from the bank. In other words, if we stepped off the boat and took 2 paces we'd walk straight into the gap between the pontoon and the bank. Fine in summer but in the depths of a dark winter night, not very pleasant – or safe. So, I put an emergency ladder in the river to escape in case of accidents.

The climate, we are told, is gentler than Burgundy where we'd been based for the previous five years. Neither the fierce, forty-degree heat of summer nor the numbing minus fifteen winters. We're roughly the same latitude of the south coast of England here but the locals here tell us that Diksmuide has its own microclimate that can be even gentler than places not far away. Nobody can remember when the river last froze over, indeed, apparently, frost is rare.

People here look prosperous without appearing to be in the rat race. They seem to have the ethos that if you win the rat race you're still a rat, so they avoid it. There is a content, gentle prosperity about the place without the manic endeavour you find in a big city. You get the feeling they are comfortable living here - having organised it just so for themselves. Most have a decent vehicle – which is probably why our rusty old thing attracts the odd glance.

The price they pay for having secure, comfortable life is that have to live within a set of rules which appear pretty strict to us as outsiders. Their existence seems regimented, particularly if it mirrors the rules and restrictions of harbour living. They have a set of rules that reads like a Tolkein trilogy. For example, they have decreed that the water is turned off at the end of October and will be turned on again on the 31st March. This is not ideal for the live-aboard. OK, we have decent sized tanks (2000 litres) but asking it to stretch for five months is asking a bit much. In any port we've lived I've joined in, helped out and generally gained the trust of the authorities. In other words, I feel I can be trusted to turn the water on and off as and when required. Here however I had to beg and plead and go through increasingly intransigent layers of bureaucracy to supply this most basic of needs. To be fair it is a bit of a palaver. The stopcock that feeds the tap from where we can fill up is in a manhole, under a heavy steel cover up on the pavement. This cock also supplies the whole of harbour three (about six taps over 200 metres). All the water taps on harbour 3 are 'winterized' at the end of October (emptied, drained and left open against frost) so they need to be shut before the stopcock can be turned on or expensive water would flow away into the river. Then the process needs to be reversed when we have finished filling up. A bit of a chore but only an hour's effort once every couple of weeks. It took a good deal of badgering to allow us to take water. Actually, there is one couple living on harbour three - have been in fact for the previous twelve years – and they had NEVER had the water turned on during the winter. They made what they had last as long as possible then cruised to Nieuwpoort to fill up – about fifteen kilometres each way!

People walk by. Because we're some way from the bank they are not too close to be intrusive, but near enough to pass the time of day. We are a bit unusual, perched out in the river, so some people look at us rather warily, but a few people chat. Dog walkers are the most communicative, otherwise those with a psychological irregularity, who recognise fellow lunatics.

Language is not as much a difficulty as we feared, because most locals speak English. Those that don't speak some French so we can chat in a third language. Not chat perhaps, communicate is more accurate.

So, we've got water, now we have to get rid of the rubbish. This has to go in specific bags. Specific in colour (which is changed from time to time) and size. The are 1.50 Euro each and considerably smaller than a normal 'bin' bag – annoyingly so. They are also printed with the name of the town you are in. Of course, recycling is a big issue, and you have to be careful not to mix things up or you will get a visit from the enviro-squad.

They don't like you working on the boat in the harbour – minor jobs are OK, but sanding and big painting jobs are not allowed. For us with an old boat that needs constant attention this is a bit of a nuisance. But, as always, there is an answer. A few hundred metres upriver is an outdoor activity business with a pontoon and we can moor there to work – for 20 Euros a day. Or go a couple of hours upriver to Fintele, previously mentioned, where we don't patronise the eel restaurant, both for budgetary and dietary reasons.

So, if you don't need water, don't generate any rubbish and don't want to work on your boat, here is perfect. To be fair, it's a friendly, safe place to be and we've been made very welcome. We have actually been accepted into their club which not only gives us preferential mooring rates but also discounts in many places throughout Flanders, harbours who are in the same Association. The likes of Bruges, Ghent and many others are half price when you present your club card. We had to appear in person before the committee before being accepted – which was a bit like a job interview, and rather nerve-wracking – but they still let us join. We have tried to mix in around the port too, helping pressure wash the pontoons and doing a spot of painting for example. Jan's even cleaned the loos on occasion.

We were invited to the Presidents New Year bash. It included the club's AGM where we were burdened with a rundown of the clubs' activities throughout the previous year. I gather they are in good shape financially with a healthy income from members and visitors alike. The overwhelming majority of The President's speech (that's our friend Walter) was lost due to language difficulties but at one stage we were pointed at and received a conservative round of applause from the gathering – presumably being welcomed as new members. What did come across was that everyone was very proud of their club and my earlier assumptions that the Belgians have little sense of humour was proved wrong as there was laughter aplenty.

The gathering was held in a very smart 'hall' within the town and once the official part was concluded, the furniture was rearranged and we were treated to a fabulous finger-buffet in addition to liquid refreshment (largely alcoholic). Jan and I got chatting (in English and French) to a father and son who were renovating their little yacht – though not in the harbour. Very pleasant they were too. We learned that the lady of the house was out at work. She is a journalist who writes for a regional newspaper and the father suggested she did a piece on us, about living on a boat on a river in winter in a strange country. Doesn't sound like it would have mass appeal does it? But apparently we and our like do generate some interest.

A week or so later the lady phoned and arranged to come and see us. She interviewed us for a couple of hours and took photographs. A pleasant lass, she politely showed some interest in my first book, A Barge at Large, and took away a proof copy to try and learn why two apparently sane individuals had chosen such a scatty life. Three weeks later we'd heard absolutely nothing and only found out that the article had appeared in the paper when one of the harbourmasters told us. He copied it for us – it was of course in Flemish so not much good, but at least part of our story is in print in a foreign land. It took four emails and seven phone calls to persuade the journalist to return my book – which she did, covered in squiggles (the book, not her).

Later in the winter, early spring actually, we were also filmed for television. There is a peculiar thing here where, during an early-evening 'magazine' programme, car-drivers are asked questions on camera, live, on a garage forecourt. If they answer a certain percentage of questions correctly, everyone giggles a bit and they are rewarded with a tank of fuel – or a part tank, I'm not sure. Well, they had decided to perform the same exercise with boats and on the day chosen for filming, we were the only boat available (or gullible enough). President Walter thought it would be good publicity for the boat club so we could hardly refuse. They didn't actually want to ask us any questions, probably thought we were too thick, no, they wanted us for 'colour'. In other words, they would film us driving into the fuel station and tying up. Footage broadcast would be the equivalent to the start of an epic film where the camera pans in over an endless savannah towards a single stagecoach way down in the valley. Our trail of engine smoke would be akin to the dusty plain thrown up by the wagon. I was a bit nervous, what with driving up the river between all the moored boats, and as far as I could see it was a lose / lose situation. If we did it well we would be on a TV channel we can't receive in a language we can't speak and get no free fuel. If I buggered anything up I would get a hefty repair bill from any number of boats and they would have something their viewers would get a good laugh at! We managed OK, glided in and tied up – pointed at by a camera and blinded by lights.

'Once more please,' said a posh lady who looked to be important.

'Again?' I asked, having thought I'd got away with it.

'We need shots from different angles.' she replied.

We actually did it six times! On each occasion we had to reverse up the river and come in again while the camera operator took footage from minimally differing angles – except when he crossed the river bridge and filmed from the other side – from where he got a perfect shot of my underpants hanging in the window. Finally, it was over. We'd probably used about thirty gallons of diesel.

'Is that a wrap? I shouted as we pulled away. At least they had the grace to giggle.

Stop Thief

I don't let Jan out that often. Historically she tends to end up in a 'situation'. Like getting stuck in a self-cleaning loo in France or ordering half of a kilo of hashish at the butchers (by mistake I might add). No, I try and keep her on a short rein, we don't want to be responsible for an international incident, after all, we quite like it here. While on a recent visit to the UK I was reacquainted with my old mate Nobby. He's getting on a bit and lives in a retirement home so periodically I write to him. He tells me is pleased to have a distraction from his daily routine – even letters from me.

Here's one relating one of Jan's shopping trips.....

Diksmuide, Flanders (Belgium if you didn't know. Or if you've forgotten!)

Dear Nobby

As you're aware Jan has a propensity for 'integrating' and making people smile while out foraging. Not in the hedgerows you understand, but while browsing shops and markets. Not that she ignores hedgerows altogether, she reckons you can find some decent plastic bags in there as long as you avoid the little black ones! Anyway, let me take you back to the run-up to Christmas here in Diksmuide. It's a late shopping day when everything stays open well into the evening.

There is a market in the main town square, both cloth-covered stalls that move from town to town daily, and a dozen semi-permanent wooden structures that are here for a couple of weeks during the height of the festive rush. The temporary stalls sell fresh meat, fish, vegetables etc., while the wooden cabins provide refreshment - beer, snacks and the like. But the atmosphere is a happy one.

Shops, both around the square and down adjoining streets are open and busy. In fact, it's great to see a town centre buzzing. It is a prosperous place and money flows over counters at a rate to which we are not accustomed.

The square looks lovely with its Christmas lights, impressive buildings and cobbled streets. Jan is on her bike (because it's nearly a kilometre from the boat) which suits me just fine as she's limited in what she can carry. She's actually a pretty good shopper, knowing both our limited budget and lack of space to put things when she gets them home. Basically, the rule is, if we buy something we have to get rid of something else.

As I write you this letter Jan is in the galley preparing some treats for Christmas day. She's just announced that she's making some potato cakes – and suddenly I'm feeling a bit juddery. Last time she made these there was nearly a catastrophe. Maybe you remember. It was when we were living at the farm in Littleborough. She bought out a couple of potato cakes with a cup of tea while I was clearing leaves. They were made with care and love but something was amiss. I'm not sure what had gone wrong but they had the consistency of plasterboard, with a worse taste. Perhaps she'd used cement instead of flour, whatever, they were not the best. I had to spit mine out. She gave a bit to the dog – who also spat it out and dashed inside for a drink.

'I'm sure these things are fine,' said Jan, 'we just need something with a bigger throat.'

At that time we rented out the adjoining field to a lady with a couple of horses. They would come and nuzzle as we sat on the wall, snuffling bits of carrot out of your pocket. Jan gave one a potato cake. It immediately started coughing and dashed off round the field kicking its back legs in the air. I don't know much about horses but I was fairly certain that this one was in some distress. It was a beautiful looking animal, sleek and light brown with a white mane and could easily have graced the stable of a wealthy Arab – until Jan gave it a cake. We dashed into the barn for a bucket of water and set off after the distressed horse. It actually came to us and did have a drink. Then with a final rasping cough and a violent shake of its head, the cake disappeared.

That was twenty years ago and she hasn't made a potato cake since – until now!? I hope this isn't my final communication.

Back in Diksmuide on the night in question, Jan fancied a coffee and cake herself, so went into the 'Butter Hall' just off the square. Butter was (and perhaps still is) big business in the town and, as the name suggests it was the place where butter was traded. That evening there was a table-top sale of knick-knacks and a cafe. While waiting in the queue Jan got talking to a couple of ladies. They were really friendly and interested that someone was living on a boat on the river during the winter – surprised indeed. They were less surprised when they discovered we were English as the 'people from the land over the sea in the west' are known to have peculiar habits. Anyway, Jan went to sit down with her brew and cake. She likes to just sit and people watch and is quite happy watching the world go by. This time however she was joined at the table by a stranger – a man.

'My wife tells me you are English and on your own,' he said.

'That's right,' replied Jan, a little warily.

'She says that you shouldn't be sitting here on your own so I've come to keep you company and have a chat.'

Jan was rather surprised, to say the least.

Turns out that this chap was President of the Belgian Brass Band Society. He'd met the leader of the Black Dyke Band in the UK and knew all about the festivals that we visited in the Pennine towns near where we used to live, in Saddleworth and Todmorden – remember? They chatted for half an hour before Jan got withdrawal symptoms and went back to her shopping.

But - how friendly is that?? Just like being back in Littleborough. She was really touched that a complete stranger took an interest in a single lass from another country – albeit under orders from his wife. Nice though eh?

Things went down-hill a bit after that.

There are some rather posh, expensive shops bordering the square and many had 'sale rails' outside. You know the sort of thing, basically a metal bar with legs on wheels.

Jan went looking for a bargain. Fortunately, she couldn't find anything so she got on her bike and moved on. Or would have done if she hadn't somehow got the rail (or one of its garments) tangled up with the bike. She set off dragging the whole rail down the pavement – much to the surprise, then amusement, of the three ladies still trying to root out a bargain. Perhaps it wasn't the subtlest bit of shoplifting you've ever seen, but once again she'd put smiles on people's faces.

I hope that Christmas isn't too traumatic and that your gout has cleared up.
Fondly
Jo

Motorhome (Wreck on wheels)

Right, as previously mentioned, we've amended our fleet of vehicles. Total age for the three is now 148 years. The boat is 110, my bicycle is 15 so, yes, our newly acquired camper van is 23! In 1992, the year Windsor Castle caught fire and the Queen was forced to pay income tax, our van rolled of the production heap. I'm not sure if there's an equation like dog-to-human years but I have to say, although it's old, it actually looks older. It didn't appear quite so mottled when we viewed it for the first time when our friends paid us a visit last November. Yes, the time of year is important because by the time they left for their campsite it was 6.30pm and dark. They'd told us during the visit that they 'wanted to get rid of it' so they could upgrade – to a wheelbarrow perhaps. Examining a new purchase in the gloom is not very smart but our friends are decent folk who wouldn't rip us off. They had just returned from a three-month trip to Portugal so the van had proved its credentials – at least we presumed they had actually travelled in the van!

We'd been toying with the idea of a camper for a while, put off primarily by budgetary limitations. Anything trouble-free (which is probably impossible to find anyway) would cost a fortune and although there are plenty of cheap alternatives around these may have serious issues, from damp or rust to knackered engines. In other words, you have to be very careful when buying something older – or be a mechanic with deep pockets. OR, do it like we have – on a wing and a prayer.

Jan has also developed an irritating alimentary condition resulting in her needing the loo at a moment's notice which is part of the reason for investing in a travelling bog. Other reasons included the possibility of trucking off south during the winter to avoid the worst of a north European winter and the opportunity to return to the UK to visit friends without having to scrounge a bed. It's OK staying with friends or family for a day or two but it can get rather difficult for both parties after a while, however well you get on with them.

Another complication was that we had a car and selling a vehicle (which is 'not new') is not that easy, particularly as we were based partly in Belgium. Anyhow the upshot was that we agreed between us to do a swap - car for camper. We agreed to pay the value differential.

Price agreed it was now down to logistics. We decided on a place for the exchange – Reims, France. I drove south for four hours in the car. My friend's journey, from the opposite direction, took six hours in the camper. I'd arrived in air-conditioned luxury having travelled at 130 kph sitting in a leather armchair listening to a six-speaker hi-fi system. I returned at 80 kph not being able to hear anything above the noise of the J5 Peugeot engine and torrential wind and rain battering my tin can. My return journey took six hours. Two-thirds of the way back, approaching the Belgian border, with the van dancing around the carriageway in the gusty winds. While ferociously sawing the faux-plastic steering wheel to avoid a nasty collision with on-rushing trucks in a contra-flow, I began to question my sanity and wondered whether I'd done the right thing! I stopped for diesel – an occurrence that was to become all too familiar as the dear old van doesn't have the best fuel economy. It's not the most aerodynamic of beasts, in fact at one point while going uphill into the teeth of a nasty squall, I had to drop down to second gear so I didn't come to a grinding halt on the motorway.

But get home I did – and that's the point. Although it's not quick, it gets you there. I have to say the front seats are very comfortable and once you get used to the idea of travelling at a maximum of 50 mph, it's really not too bad. The camper is built on a Talbot Express chassis, basically a small van. The Talbot bit is fair enough but Express is stretching the trades description act. Thinking about it, when it was built, the competition was probably horses so it would have been an express – at least when compared to a slow horse.

Inside there are two long side seats that double as beds, a shower / loo room, cooker, fridge, gas heater and plenty of storage space, largely in overhead cupboards. It's fully carpeted and finished with a mixture of light-coloured roof and wallboards and faux plastic wood-effect cupboards. Actually, inside it is pretty tidy and once you've turned off the engine, very pleasant. When people scoff I tell them, 'go on then, have a poo in your vehicle and see how you get on'!

The morning following my return is Jan's first opportunity to see the camper in all its glory – and she loves it! So, I have to love it too. She dives in and busies herself readying our acquisition for its first test trip. She cleans, polishes and hoovers, putting her own stamp on it following which I take it to the doctor to replace the two front tyres and have the spare repaired. Then I replace the gas line (that hailed from the van's birth and was consequently 18 years out of date) and replaced the fan belt that was hanging on by a thread. This latter task wasn't all that straightforward. I drove four kilometres to the fan belt shop where the helpful assistant sympathised with my van and looked up the correct replacement belt in his catalogue – a publication of some age which he found in the attic under a pile of carpets dating back to the first world war. I returned to base and removed the knackered fan belt but found it was a different width to the replacement. Of course, the van at this stage is undrivable so I cycled back to the fan belt shop to check that I actually had the right one. Unfortunately, en-route I fell off. I arrived at the shop with a variety of developing bruises and blood trickling from below my shorts from a gash on the leg. The man in the shop offered further sympathy but confirmed that the belt was indeed the right one – which meant that the belt already on the van was the wrong one.

I tested the leisure battery (that powers the lights when we're parked up) and the mains-voltage hook up – which all worked fine. I checked the fridge which appeared OK while running on mains power (it also runs on 12-volt electricity from the batteries and gas though I didn't check them – not wanting to discover a costly 'discrepancy'). I couldn't get the water heater going. No matter, we would boil a kettle on the hob (which worked fine) to wash up. I checked the loo which is a cassette-type and with which we were familiar from our narrowboat days, and that worked OK. I failed to get the room-heater going (it's gas so would probably need checking by a specialist before I blew the van up) so brought in an oil-fired radiator from the boat for heat.

I filled the drinking water tank – 65 litres, which is perfectly adequate for a few days if we didn't have a shower – which we didn't because the shower tray is cracked. I also filled the toilet's water reservoir used to flush the loo – via the electric flushing mechanism – electric flush note!!

We're parked on the cobbled road adjacent to our boat. Now the Belgians are very clean and tidy race and take a dim view of pollution of any kind. Unfortunately, under the van we could see various dribbles where overflows had done their job while I was filling up. This would all run off and dry up in no time. More worryingly there was a patch of oil under the engine which would leave a rather more permanent reminder of our stay. Our mate had told me he had accidentally overfilled the engine oil which was the reason for this dribble. In addition, there were various oily smears following my mechanical efforts. We realized that it was time to get going before the enviro-squad arrived again.

So, we set off on shake down trip, which was to be a short, one night affair. We'd planned to overnight at a pleasant looking six-berth camp site near a river – about forty kilometres distant. 'I'm going to avoid the motorways.' I announced, 'and take the scenic route.'

Flanders is very flat so wherever you go it's not that scenic, but the towns and farmland are pleasant enough. We've travelled parts of Holland and Belgium in our boat so are familiar with the lay of the land. On a boat we are 'down' in canals and rivers with a restricted view. In the camper we're perched quite high up in the cab so can see much more flat land – endless skies with church steeples and cows. We avoided not only motorways but (somehow) A and B roads too. We soon discovered that 'C' roads are largely concrete – and not that smooth either. They are laid in approximately 3-metre sections with a rubberised join between each. Hence it was a bit noisy. Driving over the concrete bits sounded like a tumble dryer full of walnuts. This racket was broken up by a regular thumps as we passed over the joins, as if someone gave the top of our tumble dryer a double tap with a rubber hammer every two seconds. It was very noisy. We could barely hear ourselves think and the dog was so frightened that it sought solace on Jan's lap.

Finally, we were back on tarmac and the noise abated somewhat so we pulled in for a break and a cup of tea to test our independence. Actually, it was rather civilized. We moved on and stopped for a late lunch at a spot that the internet had assured us was 'attractive and safe'. It was right next to a public swimming pool so it certainly wasn't quiet and the only space we could find to park was adjacent the toilet-emptying facility. Historically, when we journeyed in the car, Jan would prepare sandwiches for our journey – no matter how far we were going - hence Jan butty. Here though we could prepare everything from scratch in our van. To personalise our little domain, Jan had bought a couple of rugs. They are hairy, red things that moult worse than a dog so they will have to go – our sandwiches were getting covered in hair. We rather hoped things would improve – particularly as they charged 3 Euros for one hours electricity, a similar amount for one hundred litres of water plus eighteen Euros should we wish to stay overnight. This was no posh camp site let me tell you, just one of the many transitory stop-off points with basic facilities. Goodness know how much a smart place would charge. The dog had a good romp on a muddy field before we moved on.

We found our overnight parking spot which was located near a small boat marina. Very attractive it was too, overlooking the river (or perhaps it was a wide canal). There was one other van here. More than a van actually, a sort of posh bus, one of those with side-pods that come out hydraulically to extend the interior from big to huge. It was plugged in to two separate electricity points – perhaps one was used exclusively for its hot-tub. It was enormous and made ours look like a knackered old ant. But.....were they any happier than us? – yes, probably.

We went down to the boat club for a beer and ask whether they could accommodate our boat later in the season. We were on more familiar territory here, among boaty people. Not that our boat is particularly smart but on a comparable scale it would fit in rather better than our camper did next to the monolith. They were very helpful, cheery people who said they would make us welcome when we sailed in. Good job they couldn't see the vehicle in which we'd arrived!

We went back up to the van for supper but I had to return to the boat club to borrow a lighter because the matches we used to light the hob had fallen in the sink. Jan did a great job preparing a meal in the 'galley' and we washed up using water from a boiled kettle. You know, though basic, it was actually all rather civilized.

So, we clattered our way back to our boat in Diksmuide and our first mini adventure was over. Experiences like this are better on reflection. The more wine I consume the more amusing they appear looking back. It took about two gallons on this occasion but I finally managed a smirk.

Shopping Woes

Generally, we communicate adequately – just on the odd occasion is there is a hiccup.......

Diksmuide (Still here). Flanders (In case you've forgotten again)

Dear Nobby

Jan's been at it again. This time it was two days before Christmas.

As you well know, shopping in the period leading up to the big day can be an awful experience. It's the same the world over. Not just Christmas indeed, any time leading up to a special day, religious or not. Like back in Littleborough Nobby when they forecast snow flurries and the whole town dashes out and stocks up for Armageddon. It is often the time when good manners and common sense are done away with.

Del Haize, a large local supermarket, is packed with people, and they are harassed. Hoards are pushing and shoving, generally fraught and desperate to get it all over with. It's hot and children are squawking. It's a dreadful time of year for those that have to battle to fill trolleys with stuff they can't do without – much of which will probably go straight in the bin anyway. Christmas carols, normally the harbinger of peace and goodwill are driving people crazy and somehow make things worse. Because of the communal stress there's the feeling that someone in this seething cauldron will simply snap and spark a riot.

Enter Jan.

She chose today to end up in a bit of a tangle with a native. Many Flemish people speak English and French with near fluency. But near fluency is not fluency and some of the less common words just don't come. She was leaning over the freezer cabinet with a Belgian lady when Jan pointed to a particular packet and asked what sort of meat it was.

'Rabbit,' the lady said. 'Well nearly rabbit - but bigger.'

'Wild Boar?' asked Jan.

'Nay, Nay,' ('No' in Dutch) said the woman.

'Nay,' said Jan under her breath, pausing for a moment. 'Ah, HORSE!'

'No, No Nay,' said the woman, 'not 'Horse' neigh, I mean 'No' nay.'

'No-nay, what on earth is no-nay? Is it Pork?'

'No, a pork is not a rabbit.'

'No, I realize that.'

By now both ladies were smiling.

'It's er, got four legs,' said the lady pointing to the packet.

'Well, that narrows it down a bit,' said Jan.

And they started laughing - so loudly in fact that they attracted a bit of an audience. Jan leaned into the freezer again for a better look. Her glasses steamed up so that made them laugh more.

Then the lady's husband arrived and asked what was going on.

The Belgian lady was crying with laughter. Drying her eyes, she pointed to the packet and asked her husband what it was.

'Meat,' he said – which just seemed to make things worse. 'Like rabbit,' he added helpfully.......'but the back legs are bigger'.'

After a pause.

Kangaroo? Asked Jan.

'Nay nay,' said the husband......

.....And so it went on - by which time quite a crowd had gathered wondering what was so amusing about a cabinet full of dead meat. It was all rather infectious and before long everyone was in stitches....

'Hare!,' said a member of the audience, 'it's hare.'

'Oh yes, of course,' said Jan and the woman together.

Pause.

'We don't like hare,' said Jan......

More laughter.

As she walked towards the vegetables, where she would at least recognize things, everyone had a smile on their face. Other shoppers joked and laughed with her and, for a few people at least, this shopping trip was tolerable.

"So heere iiit iiis Merry Christmas, everybody's having fun............"

You won't get this till after Christmas so I hope everything was tolerable. I know a lot of your fellow residents tend to fall asleep before lunch so I hope you have someone to exchange cards and presents with. Did you get my card? Hopefully it is OK! Remember when Jan sent Carly a Dutch 'birthday card' when we were living in Holland? Carly put the script in Google translate - turns out it said, 'In Deepest Sympathy'.

We're thinking of you and hope to see you before long.

Happy New Year.

Fondly

Jo

Early one Sunday morning I was out walking the hound down a cinder track when, behind a fence, I spotted a lady in red pyjamas. She'd come out of a tent, one of about a dozen, to do whatever a camper does at 6.30 in the morning. I asked her what was going on. 'I'm going for a pee,' she said.

I hadn't really meant to enquire of her habits. I told her I was more interested why she and her companions were tenting in a field.

'Oh,' she laughed, 'we're here for the BBQ weekend.'

We'd seen various goings on round and about and later that day while on the boat, Jan was tantalised by a fragrant fog drifting our way. 'That's making me smell hungry,' she said.

Perhaps it didn't come out quite right but she was (nearly) spot on, there was a good smell. Across the river in the shadow of the menacing Ijzertower, the Low Countries Annual BBQ Championships was under way. From our viewpoint the activities were largely hidden behind the high riverbank but smoke from twenty-five or thirty BBQs drifted over Flanders, dimming the bright, autumn sun.

We had to go and investigate this. The event spanned two large Flanders fields, one housed the BBQs, beer marquee and seating and the other ancillary marquees. Entry was free but if you wanted to actually taste anything you had to pay. You couldn't pay cash though. You had to leave field one and buy tokens (at 2 euros each) from a shed in field two, then return to exchange the tokens for a bite to eat in field one. I'm still a bit mystified why we couldn't just pay cash in field one but there you go. All a bit sneaky really. Entry to the fields was free but, here as anywhere, there's no such thing as a free lunch. Not only do you have to buy tokens to pay for food, you have to march to and fro to buy them, thereby giving you an appetite. One token would get you a taste of BBQ rib, 2 tokens a forked pork bap. If you're greedy like me, it could get rather expensive over the course of three hours, particularly if you need a reviver in the form of a specialist ale or two.

I've never visited a BBQ Championship before and I can safely say the not a single one my charred offerings (created over the previous thirty years) would have won any prizes here. Some of the food looked fabulous - more akin to things that would grace a top restaurant rather than a field.

Competition entries were put on a tiered shelving for judging and Joe public was held back by crowd control barriers. The shelving was over ten metres long and had four tiers so there were many offerings. By the look of it each entrant could submit four dishes which were all displayed on square china white plates. I don't know who won because at judging time I was in bed with stomach ache.

Not only was there a vast variety of food but also a wacky array of equipment. There was a VW camper van completely covered in astroturf with a large side window like an eco-warriors ice-cream van. Next door twelve chickens roasted on a spit above a huge pan of charcoal. 'Low and Slow Smokin' Boar 11' was a monster. A six-wheel monolith built from black steel with chrome trim. Big enough to cater for a rock festival, it created enough smoke to cause climate change. Then there was an English participant, called Miss Piggy's BBQ who looked to be cooking on oil drums. From further afield, Zach Murray's 'Swine and Wine' blew in from Lynchburg, Tennessee. A truly international event.

In field two there was a Morris Minor shooting break, the one with wooden trim, promoting whiskey in Belgium and the inevitable bouncy castle for the kids. A septet dressed in waistcoats and bowler hats (and trousers) marched about playing trad jazz, a jolly distraction probably designed to ease the frustration of having to buy tokens.

And there were hundreds and hundreds of people milling about with nothing better to do on a sunny Sunday than enjoy themselves. What a pleasant hour or two.

Uncle Percy

Diksmuide, Flanders

Dear Nobby

Remember I mentioned Jan's Uncle Percy, well, I never have told you the full story, but I'm inspired to do so as we're in Flanders, so here we are.......

A couple of years ago, in May 2013 in fact, we were driving from Calais back to St. Jean de Losne. En route we stopped at The Beaumont-Hamel Newfoundland Memorial to pay our respects to Percy. He is buried there having died on 1st July 1916 – the first day of the Battle of the Somme.

He was fighting with the Border Regiment alongside the Newfoundland Regiment as part of the 29th British Division.

While researching her ancestry Jan came across Percy, her Dad's brother (you remember Jack), which led her to his grave. She has subsequently discovered that, two years prior to his death, he was fighting in Flanders, mere metres from where we currently moor our boat. She came across the following on the Ypres Battlefields forum:

He (Percy) wrote a letter dated November 1914 from Brand Lodge Hospital, Malvern which contained some uncensored details.

"On the morning of the 29th October the battle had been in progress for 36 hours, and the whole of that time we had been holding a position near Diksmuide (Belgium) firing at each other the whole time, and we could not advance as we were not strong enough, and we were waiting for reinforcements which never

came. In the meantime, the Germans got up their reinforcements and they came on in great masses until they were 50 yards from our trench, and to save ourselves we had to charge, and the mix up lasted about half an hour. Then off went the Germans as fast as they could go with us hard on their heels. During the mix up I got my arm ripped up,. This happened about 11 am and at 4pm I got a bullet through the leg. After that I knew nothing more until it was quite dark and all was silent. At first I could not tell what had happened, then I tried to rise, but I could do nothing beyond getting on my knees. I then looked round and found the direction I had to take to get back to a field hospital, at least two miles, so I started crawling, rolling, anything to get back. At last I became exhausted again and lost consciousness. The next I knew I was laid on some straw in a temporary hospital in Ypres, and I was told that I was to be sent to England that day. I am getting on splendidly, so I should be home soon"

In a further letter dated 14th November he wrote:

"I shall not be home quite as soon as I expected, because I have had to undergo another operation".

On the 16th November he had four bullets extracted from his leg.

We might have expected that with such injuries he would remain in England but no. On Saturday the 1 July 1916, Littleborough (Lancashire, England) born 24-year-old Sergeant 10358 Percy Kershaw, 1st Bn Border Regiment was killed in action in France, (his Bns objective on the 1st July was the capture of Beaumont Hamel, his Bn suffered 575 casualties, Beaumont Hamel was eventually captured 13 November 1916) He is buried in Hawthorn Ridge Cemetery No 2, Auchonvillers, Somme, France Grave Number A. 2.

It's an extraordinary coincidence that Diksmuide, mentioned in Percy's letter, is where we are moored this winter. A further coincidence is that Diksmuide is twinned with Ellesmere, Shropshire, where we spent the last 15 years of our time in England. Jan was speaking to an elderly gentleman the other day who lives in one of the apartments overlooking the port and is a former town councillor here. He was one of the delegation who travelled to Shropshire and officially opened Diksmuide Avenue in Ellesmere.

We're not sure exactly where Percy was fighting in 1914 but we can be sure it was close by. There is a preserved trench a few hundred metres north, probably a replica of where Percy and his colleagues spent terrified hours. It's now a 'tourist' spot known as The Trench of Death and hundreds of visitors come to glimpse the past and try to imagine the horror and claustrophobia of life in a filthy trench.

The Beaumont-Hamel Newfoundland Memorial site is the largest area of The Somme battlefield to have been preserved and one of only a few where you can see trenches. The 74-acre site was purchased by Newfoundland in 1921 and was one of six Newfoundland memorial sites set up following the first world war. (Newfoundland was a dominion of the British Empire at this time till it became part of Canada in 1949). The memorials themselves are huge bronze caribou that stand atop mounds of Newfoundland granite. The caribou stand facing their former foe with their heads held high in defiance, not dissimilar to the lion atop the Menen Gate in Ypres. The site also contains three commonwealth cemeteries including Hawthorne Ridge Number 2 Cemetery, site of Percy Kershaw's grave.

The day we visited it was raining. Puddles had begun to form in the (now) grass-filled bomb craters and trenches but we don't even begin to get an idea of the nightmare it must have been for Percy and his comrades amidst the mud and murder in 1916.

Just out of interest, my regular dog walk route is along a cinder path that was a single-track railway during the war carrying supplies between Diksmuide and Nieuwpoort. It's now a cycle / walking path along which you can see the remains of various fortifications left over from a hundred years ago. I was walking the dog one day last winter when I spotted something in the field by the path. Just a glint I got but when I picked it up I realised it was the nose of a bomb. About four inches long and similar in diameter, it was very muddy and heavy for its size. When I cleaned it up I looked it up on the internet and found that it's the nose of a shrapnel bomb. Judging by the size of the nose the full bomb would have been about 18 / 24 inches long. The whole thing would have been pretty weighty and the thought of one of these landing nearby is awful. I'll show you when I get back. Might do for a door stop and keep that annoying, white-haired chap out of your room!

   Fondly

   Jo

How to win Friends.....

We went to Brussels in the car – mistake. On a normal day it's busy, but we chose the day they were practising for the funeral of a female member of the Belgian Royal Family. She had actually died I might add, it wasn't just a random practice. Carrying out a trial funeral with the protagonist watching on from a bedroom window would likely be considered a touch insensitive.

Brussels is a major tourist, financial and political hub so is not only crowded but also a target for fanatics. The authorities had to be sure that dignitaries were safe while attending the funeral so they had a dry run. What it meant was that, because the proposed route was closed to traffic, the rest of the city centre was gridlocked.

Being stuck in a jam is a leveller. We, in our rusty-bonneted Peugeot, rubbed wing mirrors with a lot a fancy motors driven by people who thought they were significant. It was a seething mass of eurocratic self importance – and horrid.

While stuck, a very worrying wisp of steam drifted up from the font of the car. I had to keep turning the engine off before re-staring to move another few feet. If the dear old thing had packed up here, recovery would have been nigh impossible. Thankfully we escaped.

Fortunately, the chap we were meeting at the Cypriot Embassy was also stuck in traffic so when we both arrived an hour late we could bemoan the inconsiderate timing of the poor lady's demise. It was a peculiar meeting within a sea of Brussels suits. We in boat attire, he in classic Mediterranean 'official' gear, wrinkled trousers and black leather jacket.

I went to the Belgian capital a second time, on this occasion to the British Embassy to have my passport extended by twelve months. A useful service this for anyone who cocks up the usual renewal procedure. It's done in a couple of hours and is free. This time I went on the train which was much less stressful. Once again I was dressed 'boaty' in shorts, T-shirt and rucksack. I was eyed suspiciously by two soldiers guarding the embassy entrance, who cocked their automatic rifles as I approached.

While I waited for my passport I wandered through the adjacent Parc du Cinquintaire (or Jubel Parc - Jubilee Park). So named because, commissioned in 1880, it celebrates fifty years of Belgian independence. Magnificent it is too. The centrepiece of an impressive U-shaped arcade is the Triumphal Arch built in 1905 to replace a previous temporary version. The buildings house museums including the Royal Military Museum and AutoWorld. I'd had my fill of military misery in Diksmuide so browsed the Auto museum where I discovered some wonderful vintage vehicles almost as old as our camper.

Diksmuide, Flanders (Belgium – you'd forgotten hadn't you)

Dear Nobby

You've done your fair share of travelling so you know it's always nice to integrate and make friends in a foreign land. When locals smile and wave you feel part of things. Recently we were visiting English friends on their boat in Bruges when it obliquely led to my befriending a pair of natives. Bruges by the way is an amazing place, one of the premier tourist destinations in Europe. Have you been? I'm not sure. William Caxton of printing fame originated here. Not that you're bothered about that, except that without him your Daily Telegraph would still be engraved on a stone tablet. Anyhow, more importantly my driver's side headlamp stopped working. It's Tuesday afternoon in early December, and 4.00 pm so we haven't much time to get back to Diksmuide before the light fades. It's a 35 minutes drive and unless we hurry I'll need my headlights. I was loathed to try and change the bulb in the gathering dusk (by a busy road) in case I made a mess of it and wrecked the whole car. So, we set off back and just about made it, barely legally.

The following morning I dismantled the headlamp cluster (yes, on my own!) and checked spare bulb kit (the carrying of which is a compulsory requirement in Belgium). I discovered that the bulb didn't fit. Good job I hadn't tried to change it the previous evening.

I reassembled the headlamp and drove down to local Peugeot dealers in our very scabby 11-year-old 406 to purchase a couple of new bulbs. In addition to some nasty rusty patches there is a gouge in the rear quarter where, in my absence, it was attacked by a mechanical digger in Burgundy. I parked in front of the showroom but hidden away behind a big white van so nobody could see me.

I raised the bonnet, dismantled the assembly again and removed the bulb. Carrying the defective item, I entered a pristine emporium – a serene world of shiny new motors, soothing piano music and the smell of 'autumn pine' floor cleaner. Reminded me of the dining room in your place actually, without the cars.

There were two very smartly dressed ladies seated behind the desk ready to attend to my every need. Each wore designer clothes and enough jewellery to stock a modest shop and both had beautifully coiffured hair. Their enthusiasm was tempered when they saw my saggy jogging bottoms. A T-shirt promoting an American Bourbon and my mucky hands didn't help either. My running shoes (now used exclusively as walking shoes) squeaked rather as I approached which got the ladies attention - as if with each step I was squishing one of their pet gerbils. They had every right to be wary but, despite my mottled appearance, they barely missed a beat and were politeness personified.

'Good morning, could I have two of these please,' I said, handing over the broken bulb.

'Certainly Sir.'

Lady one disappeared through a door into the storeroom while lady two engaged me in polite conversation. 'Could we interest you in a replacement vehicle perhaps?' she asked, waving a bangle-strewn arm in the direction of the gleaming new cars – mainly because the van had departed leaving my sorry looking lump in full view. I smiled politely.

'That will be 26 Euros please,' said Lady one on her return.

'Ah,' I said. 'I'll just take one thank you.'

I had a limited budget and had mistakenly thought that 20 Euros would be enough for 2 bulbs.

I paid and went to change the bulb in the car park and reassembled everything.

The head-light still didn't work.

Drawing on my vast knowledge of vehicle electrics I referred to the vehicle manual, took out the requisite fuse and returned to the smart ladies. 'Could I have one of these please?'

'Certainly Sir.'

I paid (1.09 Euros) and went outside to replace the fuse.

Damn headlight still didn't work!

Following a deal of head scratching I discovered the problem. I'd change the wrong bulb!! Don't smirk! Remember when you did the tappets on your old Morris and had all those bits left over when you'd finished. You're no expert yourself, so stop grinning!

Turns out there are two identical bulbs in each cluster you see, and I had replaced a perfectly good main-beam lamp in error.

I returned to my new friends in the showroom, who this time pretended to be engaged on their telephones. I suspect they were speaking with each other discussing how much of an idiot I was.

'You know on my first visit you threw that old bulb away?' I asked, when Lady one had finished on the phone.

'Yeeees.'

'Do you think I could possibly have it back? I changed the wrong bulb you see and, well……' I petered out.

Lady one was patently none too pleased about having to go and delve in the store-room bin – but she did, handing it over with fore-finger and thumb, rather like she was handling one of the dead gerbils I'd killed earlier.

I changed the bulb and – finally, it worked!

So, I've ended up with the main-beam bulb in the headlamp slot and a brand-new bulb in main-beam slot – despite the fact that the main beam was working perfectly well in the first place. I don't have a spare bulb but I do have a spare fuse - just in case anything else goes wrong.

I've also befriended two rather nice ladies.

There you go - that's how you win friends and integrate in a foreign land. Easy eh?

Sorry to hear about your mate John. He was a great character, I'm sure you miss him. Hopefully see you before too long.

Fondly

Jo

Camper Battle

Battling around in our old camper is all part of our journey. It may offer a foretaste of our future, who knows. If our recent sortie to England is anything to go by we are, at least, in for some interesting times.....

So, as the initial camper trip had been so effortless (!), we were full of confidence and felt ready to tackle a journey to the UK. She's a mottled, dented beast who I've affectionately called Van Wrinkle. (The previous owners, our friends, called her Me Van Oui, which is rather clever but we needed to put our own stamp on her – but not too hard or we may go through the floor!). Although we won't be travelling in air-conditioned luxury, in one way there is less pressure as we can take our time – we have all we need with us and if we want to stop off somewhere we can.

Despite the low value of the camper, it costs nearly three times as much as the car to take the below-channel tunnel. We really have to take the tunnel because the dog is with us. On the ferry he has to remain alone in the vehicle while we travel 'upstairs' and if we left him alone for too long he may have 'rearranged' the soft furnishings when we return. Actually, it's a good job we've got plenty of storage so we can accommodate all the paperwork needed for dear old Tache in addition to a box or ten of wine for personal consumption.

We had arranged to stay at our friends' house (sleeping in the van on their drive but plugged into electricity) near Holbeach, Lincolnshire (four hours from Folkestone in the van, three in a normal vehicle). They are friends we met while boating but who have now sold up to live on land permanently. Mike is a very useful man to know and proved it once again when he found the nozzle where we pump up the air suspension on the van. We didn't even know we had air suspension! We could see the back end was a bit low but presumed it was designed like that so it could prowl the highways looking like a German Shepherd patrol dog. This lack of air and low rear end probably explained why there was such a dreadful din while driving over concrete roads - the van was probably just sitting on the rear axle.

The modification made a huge difference during our onward journey to our former home town, Littleborough, Lancashire, where we'd booked into a campsite near Hollingworth Lake (a five-hour trip with five stops for variously, 'members ablutions' and diesel). In my youth I used to run round the lake – 2.2 miles in about 15 minutes. Now I walk round in about an hour and a half. The site is £15 per night including electric / water / loo emptying and a wonderful view of the Pennine Hills. It's mid-April so a bit draughty but we park allowing us to extend out built-in awning (yes! we have an awning) and be sheltered from the wind by the van. I wound the awning out from the side of the van so we could sit on our rusty deckchairs in splendid isolation in our field. I had known we had an awning and had tested it on the road in Belgium, the one where we'd dribbled. Here I began to wind it out but a car came along so I wound it in again. I wound it out for a second time but a lorry arrived, so in it went again – and there it stayed while I went for a brew to recover. We also have side and front panels, ground sheets and bags of various poles and pegs – another time maybe.

We'd not been there long and, though I say it myself, we looked pretty impressive supping tea under our awning – until another van arrived. Another huge van – like another bus. No side pods this time but this was long enough to accommodate a tennis court so it didn't need them. Actually, the guy with the van was very friendly and it turns out it wasn't his van at all. His was being modified – and was even bigger! The reason for this surfeit of vans is that he owns a motorhome company. Many of these big ones are bought by motocross riders who want a garage in the back of the van, and a comfortable home while travelling from venue to venue.

The guy was respectful and chatty – he owns a camper-van business after all and I may be a future customer, if our finances improve – drastically. He did (politely) say that our van, although 'entry level', was probably worth more than we had paid for it, 'you'd probably get about seven grand for it on Gumtree,' he said. I showed him the back corner where someone had obviously had a disagreement with a wall and the panels were in a mess, 'well, it's still worth over five grand,' he said. The following day I had my own disagreement with an unrelated wall, thereby damaging the other rear corner. That evening over a beer he sympathised, 'It's probably worth about what you paid for it now.'

This must be some sort of record – we've lost four thousand quid in 24 hours!

I've since repaired all this carnage with aluminium checker plate and rivets. In fact, the repaired bits are probably stronger than the rest of it. Should we have an accident, the only two bits left standing would be the rear corners. There is no ingress of water – which is quite remarkable.

As I've said, our van is slow. Our neighbour's monstrosity had a big V10 engine (with lots of other numbers followed by 'turbo') and would do 110 Kph comfortably. Ours does 80 Kph on a good day. We have done about 800 kilometres since buying the van and have only managed to overtake three things. The first occasion was one for celebration indeed – even if it was a 50cc motor-scooter into a head wind.

The field we are in here in Littleborough is about an acre and a half – large, with plenty of electricity points. There is a rudimentary loo block in one corner near the sluice and water point. During our first evening a smart little car arrived. It parked across the field as far away from the toilet as possible. Two rather smart people got out and erected a rather smart little tent. It took about a minute to erect, it just seemed to spring into action. Nothing like the efforts of my youth when a bewildering array of poles and bits of canvas took a good half hour and it still ended up flopping about in the breeze. Their location obviously caused a disagreement because the couple could be heard yelling at one another well into the night. Periodically the lady would troop some distance across the field to the loo block and back before another row broke out.

I am an early riser usually up before 6.00 am. The following morning the smart little car had gone, and there was an ominous silence from the smart little tent. Three days later the tent was still there but nobody had seen any sign of life. The camp site owner, a conscientious soul, became alarmed and actually went to investigate to see if one smart person had done for the other. Fortunately, the tent was empty – it had just been abandoned. Camping, it seems, is not for everybody.

The real reason we are in the UK is to buy a couple of small terraced houses to rent out. Now I'm sure many of you have put the house up for sale and understand the effort that goes in to ready them for each potential purchaser. Imagine the vendor's horror when we pull up outside in Van Wrinkle. They probably think we are looking for somewhere to squat. Despite our mottled demeanour we are actually (reasonably) decent folk and we surprised one vendor by putting an offer in straight away – albeit a low one. They were so surprised that they accepted. (It was subsequently lowered further when we discovered the house needed a new roof).

Finding the second one has not proved as easy – vendors selfishly holding out for close to the asking price. So, we widened our search away from our chosen town of Littleborough. This involved crossing the Pennines into West Yorkshire and little former mill towns around Halifax and Huddersfield. There are some cheap properties, mainly in areas with a high immigrant population. Lots has been said about this but the more I see, the more I like the diversity of these places. If you're into Asian or oriental food for example, it's wonderful. I tend to ask around as to the preferred 'curry-house' and often find that the scruffiest-looking places turn out some terrific food. I always chat with the folks who run them, often finding they are second or third generation immigrants who have grafted to get where they have, often under some duress. I found one such place in Hipperholme, between Halifax and Brighouse, where we stayed on a magical little campsite. The proprietor of the take-away was a really nice guy and he and his two assistants cooked up a fabulous curry for me. The outside of the place was mottled but, on recommendation, I gave it a go. The guy was originally from Bradford (which in itself wasn't a surprise – and we laughed when I told him so) and we chatted about a variety of things including the National Media Museum in his home town that I had visited many years ago (when it had a more cumbersome name), and Bradford City Football Club, over whom (like many football supporters) he despaired. Mind you, he felt better when I told him my local team was Rochdale. 'Aye, there's always someone worse off than you,' he sympathised in his Indo / Yorkshire accent. What a nice guy he was.

The camp site we're staying at is big enough for 6 vans, is slightly scruffy and has no shower block. Any deficiency is soon forgotten because the site is attached to the Halifax Steam Brewing Company. The business started in 1999 when David Earnshaw started brewing Cock O' the North beer in his garden shed using an untidy assortment of equipment. A year later the brewery got its first dedicated brewery in the form of a red portacabin (like a site hut on a building site). Today it brews in part of the factory adjacent the camp site and there is a purpose-built 'tap-hole' (bar) called the Cock 'O The North bar which serves a rotation of 180 beers through 8 hand-pumps. What an absolute delight for the visiting camper!!

If you want to try all eight beers on one evening you can have one of each in 1/3-pint glasses for a pound a go. Thereafter you can choose your favourite and have a few of them at a very reasonably £2.75 a pint.

I met a gregarious Irish chap while there with whom I shared a few stories. He told me that back in his village a few people owned Lada Rivas, the 'entry-level' car from Russia. I pointed to Van Wrinkle and told him I knew all about entry level. The Lada Riva had similar aerodynamic properties to the camper but with more rust. My Irish mate was heralded as the unluckiest Riva driver in the village - because his actually overheated. 'Nobody else could get theirs started!' he told me.

We found no houses to suit in Yorkshire so set off back over the Pennines where we found another wreck and had our offer accepted. Now we have to wait around for the solicitors to inflate their bills so decide to set off and visit some friends. But before we headed off Jan went to the local doctor's surgery to register as a new patient - and managed to cause chaos. She'd seen the doc and was that relieved to have it all over and done with she exited the surgery via the fire door by mistake. She found herself standing in the back garden with all the alarms going off. By the time she got round to the front door there was a full evacuation under way. Everybody was panicking to get out while Jan was trying to shove them all back through the door looking like a woman in need of a psychiatrist, 'nooo, it's me. I did it. Nooo, don't leave!'

Shrewsbury was our first stop. A lovely, wealthy market town where we had briefly lived a few years previously. The natives were wholly unprepared for the arrival of our untidy old camper jostling for position among Range Rovers and smart German saloons. We trundled into town sounding like a convoy of tanks on cobbled streets in a Belgian village during the war. The grumbling, rattling and squeaking crescendoed as we approached and alarmed locals, many not in their first flush of youth, dived for cover. As we neared the good folk of Shrewsbury turned down their hearing-aids and disappeared into bomb-shelters. As we park up, waste products dribble alarmingly onto the road. Fortunately, our toilet is a sealed unit so the locals are not to know that the rivulets are from our freshwater tank. 'NOT pee-pee,' we tell them. Unconvinced they retreat further.

When we stop Tache the dog leaps out of the door gnashing and yelping, relieved to have been released from his private hell. He then shows them what proper wee-wee is, against a rubbish bin. We actually came across a bin in France that would have been ideal in this situation as it was advertising a singer-songwriter called Dick Rivers – I kid you not!

If bystanders thought the noise of our arrival was bad they should try a stint inside the van. By some extraordinary quirk of physics, the internal racket is greater when the windows are closed. And it shakes about a bit so we go round tightening screws daily but it always sounds like the thing is coming apart at the seams. Things have improved since we sorted out the suspension but all the loose items rattle around. Imagine driving your kitchen over a corrugated iron roof and you will get the idea. Everything loose is in drawers and cupboards, if they weren't safely stored, utensils would fly around the cabin like a swarm of lethal, sharp-edged hornets inside a lavatory cubicle.

We couldn't actually find anywhere to park in town, partly because our van is too high for the car park barriers so ended up a few hundred yards away across the River Severn. Returning to the van from the town centre we were getting drenched in a torrential downpour. Tache was not happy - pulling on his lead and stopping every now and then to have a shake. We let him loose and he moved smartly ahead and walked right beside a lady with an umbrella! Not daft is he? The lady was a bit surprised to have a strange dog sharing her brolly but it gave everyone a good laugh.

We moved on to our friend's house. The family includes our two godchildren. Now we, as godparents, are supposed to offer spiritual uplift and personal support during the children's formative years. So, when Uncle Jo and Aunty Jan arrived driving a skip it appeared that assistance should be going the other way. Fortunately, the 12-year-olds are developing quite nicely without interference and being technologically savvy, were able to help us with things electronic – like getting the telly working. We parked in their driveway and plugged in our oil radiator to stave of the ferocious Shropshire weather. The children are Tom and Molly and we love them to bits. Mum and Dad are OK too!

Then we moved on to other friends nearby where we had to put a couple of house-bricks under the wheels on their steep driveway to prevent our steed careering out into the main road. It's OK actually because anything dribbling out from under the van runs away smartly into the mains sewers. John and Audrey are fine folk who have visited us on our old boat in Belgium and are amazed that we have found something even more knackered in which to travel the globe.

These folks are all friends we made when we lived nearby about 12 years ago so we have plenty of amusing stuff to talk about. I don't know if they actually enjoy seeing us again but we enjoy seeing them and it's passing the time!

So now we head up to Ormskirk to annoy another set of friends and stay with them in their park-home lodge. Al and Ju were friends we made while narrowboating but unfortunately they have had to give that up due to ill health. Their lodge is on a massive private plot and very homely. En route we bought a dog-carrier. It's a canvas thing on a metal frame. We thought the dog may feel more at home in the van if he had his own personal space. He didn't – at least initially. It's the same size as his metal one on the boat where he sleeps happily for eight hours a night. Unfortunately, we'd only had this one three hours when I ran over it with the van. There was a nasty rumbling, snappy noise as it was flattened and as I got out it was partly curled up within a wheel arch. Being of flimsy construction it was unable to withstand three tons of camper. The only consolation was that the dog wasn't in it! With some wooden dowel and duck-tape we managed to effect some sort of repair but our £40 investment would never again realise that sort of money.

Jan and I took a trip into nearby Southport and felt quite at home in our camper in this seaside town. We were aiming for Matalan to buy some undergarments (Marks and Spencer are not what they were you know). We took a wrong turn and somehow ended up in the delivery bay – where we actually fitted in quite well in our van, and being Saturday, it was nice and quiet. So, we paused for a cuppa before going shopping. We actually had quite a holiday feel about us so I had a Kentucky Fried Chicken and Jan had something from MuckDonalds.

We left the posh end of Lancashire and returned to Oldham where Jan had found another campsite associated with a pub. This was a former pub bought by a great guy called Steve and he'd turned the big back garden into a site. Very cosy it was too and Steve and his wife Julie were really pleasant, helpful people. To be frank it's not the most salubrious area of Oldham (is there one?) but we're in a little Oasis – and there's a fully functioning pub just across the road. It's extraordinary the places you find, by accident really, and the campers who share the site with us are all up for a chat and a giggle. Owner Steve is also a mechanic who used to run his own garage. He now repairs vehicles for people, even has a hydraulic ramp in his back garden. While reversing up a steep slope a few days ago an appalling smell erupted from below our van. I was riding the clutch and thought I had burned it out. Fearing an expensive repair, I asked Steve to have a look but thankfully he pronounced it fit and well. To be honest the vans systems are really put to the test around this area – it is mighty hilly and our dear old steed does struggle rather on the steep bits.

While here we met a caravanner, a man from Birmingham not to be messed with. He told us he'd been stopped for speeding by the police. They pulled in front of him, according to the guy, 'in a dangerous manner.' They tried to prosecute him but it was all turned on its head when he sued the police for dangerous driving! He'd used footage from his dash-board camera as proof. Then he'd had a moment the previous evening in the local Chinese take-away. The owner had shouted at one of his assistants and behaved in a bullying manner towards her. So, our Brummie threw a pepper-pot at him and told him to stop acting like Chairman Mao! Luckily it started raining and I could escape to our van before he found something to throw at me.

Steve has a huge dog, a Bordeaux Mastiff. 'It's soft as putty,' said Steve. It was a lovely light brown thing but really did look rather threatening. While I was sitting in the van reading a book, Tache let off one of his 'stream of howls' and disappeared through the driver's window. The next thing I knew half a ton of French dog was hurtling across the camp site chased by our diminutive terrier!

Back in Belgium.....

Diksmuide, Flanders

Dear Nobby

It was as good to see you last week. You don't look any worse than you did when we first met thirty years ago – not that that is over-encouraging! Did you ever keep that bloke with the hair awake long enough to finish that game of chess? You did make me smile when you told me the only reason he'd taken up the game was because it involved porn and queens! You seem to be developing a sense of humour – at long last.

Anyhow, I told you we would try and make the most of things in our last weeks here, but here is an account of a trip we took before Christmas. Not amusing this tale and it's perhaps a bit formal, largely because it deserves to be. This was a special outing......

Reminders of the bloody history of Flanders are all around us. It is a peaceful, prosperous area now but residents and visitors alike are not allowed to forget the past, indeed are encouraged to remember it. We are no exception and yesterday we visited one of the most poignant memorials of them all.....

Ypres, 6.45 pm, Tuesday 16th December 2014.

The town's main square is dominated by the imposing, impressive Cloth Hall. Set in the south-western corner of the square. It is 125 metres wide and sits, massive, below a 70-metre bell tower. Originally medieval, it was, and still is, a testament to the wealth of Flemish cloth merchants. The original building (as much of the town) was utterly destroyed during the First World War but between 1933 and 1967 it was rebuilt as close to the original design as possible using money paid by Germany in reparations. It is subtly floodlit and this evening looks festive amid surrounding Christmas lights and decorations.

The square is bordered by many other wonderful buildings, three and four storeys high, with steeply pitched, grey tile roofs. Many are now cafes, restaurants and shops. In front of the Cloth Hall, as in Diksmuide, semi-permanent wooden market stalls have been erected for the Christmas period and youngsters noisily cavort on and around a temporary ice rink. The restaurants and cafes are busy but many visitors are drawn to Ypres for one reason only.

Five hundred metres from the Cloth Hall, up Meenestraat off the south eastern corner of the square, is the Menen Gate.

Its location is symbolic. During the war, Meenestraat led many soldiers out of town to the battlefields from where many would never return. The memorial is white, built from reinforced concrete faced with Euville stone and red brick. The interior, known as the Hall of Memory, is barrel vaulted and single spanned to allow cars and pedestrians to pass in and out of the town on the cobbled street.

The Menen Gate was unveiled on 24th July 1927 by Field Marshal Plumer, President of the Ypres League. Portland Stone panels adorn the Hall of memory. The lower level, staircases, upper level and loggias are where the names of 54,896 soldiers are engraved. They are British and Commonwealth soldiers whose bodies have never been found or were unable to be identified, so have no known grave – collectively they are known as The Missing.

At the opening ceremony, Plumer said of these soldiers, "They are not missing – they are here."

This evening, as have millions before us, it is our turn to pay our respects.

We walk towards the monument in the company of people of all ages who chat quietly. As we approach, our eyes are drawn inevitably to the floodlit gate which straddles the road down which we pass.

The Menen Gate is one of the most famous memorials in the world but is not triumphalist. It is without doubt impressive, but it serves mightily, yet modestly, as a fitting memorial to some of the many thousands who lost their lives in the most brutal of wars. I am not a military man (nor I suspect are the vast proportion of visitors) but I pause to think what this place really represents. Nearly 55,000 soldiers – incredible. I've seen first-hand the muddy, clinging earth these soldiers endured and the thought of living and fighting and dying there is appalling. I've read many times about the price these soldiers paid and the debt we owe, but for me, it's only by coming here that I really begin to feel it.

The most senior soldier commemorated here is Brigadier General Charles Fitzclarence VC who died on 12th November 1914. To World War One veterans he became known as 'GOC (General Officer Commanding) Menen Gate.' He had won his Victoria Cross fifteen years previously for three actions of gallantry during the Boer War. He was 49 when he died fighting alongside his men, the vast majority of whom were far younger. As with all the other soldiers here his body was never found but he is immortalised and will forever keep watch over his comrades.

By strange coincidence the Brigadier died within two weeks of my wife's uncle Percy being injured fighting near Diksmuide, 20 kilometres away.

High on the eastern end of the gate is a single engraved panel dedicated to those without a known grave. Above this is the sculpture of a lion, lying down with his head raised. He is looking away from the town towards the battlefields.

Each evening the traffic is halted by the local police for the Last Post. The ceremony has been conducted here every night at 8.00 pm since 2nd July 1928 except during World War Two when Belgium was under German occupation. During that period, the ceremony was held at Brockwood Military Cemetery, Surrey, England. On the evening that Polish forces liberated Ypres during the

Second World War, the ceremony was resumed at the Menen Gate despite the fact that heavy fighting was still taking place in other parts of the town.

There are perhaps three hundred of us taking it in, some talking quietly – English, Dutch (or Flemish) and French I recognize, but there are other languages that I can't pick up.

Beneath the arch an unseen announcer asks for quiet and requests that we refrain from applauding at the conclusion of the ceremony. Each evening, during this period that commemorates the hundred-year anniversary of World War One, personal homage is paid to two soldiers who died on that particular date. Listening to the stories of two individuals somehow re-enforces the personal aspect of why we are here.

Following this five-minute eulogy, the Last Post is played.

Volunteer buglers from the local fire brigade play this haunting refrain beautifully.

The melody echoes within the memorial arch, touching each name engraved on the walls.

The sound dies away and a young female soldier marches to centre stage, stands in the absolute silence and says:

> They shall not grow old, as we that are left grow old:
> Age shall not weary them, nor the years condemn.
> At the going down of the sun and in the morning,
> We will remember them.

The words are one verse of a longer poem called 'For the Fallen' written by Laurence Robert Binyon and anyone not moved by them must be made from the stone of the memorial itself.

A wreath is laid by two young soldiers and there are a few moments silence before we all drift away, much subdued.

I read recently that the only good to come from war is friendship. Perhaps that's true. But my, what a price to pay.

Fondly

Jo

Back to Blighty

We've joined the Talbot Owners Club – yes, there is one. It's a thriving community that offers assistance to the hundreds of people that have an ancient van like ours. Often in excess of twenty years old they are like old cars but, because of all the on-board systems, there are more things to go wrong. When you see one parked at the side of the road after something has failed, often in a cloud of smoke, there are numerous savvy Talbot owners ready with helpful advice. People take a huge pride in their vans – we haven't quite reached that stage yet but she's growing on us. As I write the steering has developed a whine and the exhaust is grumbling so I'll go in search of help soon no doubt.

TOC (Talbot Owners Club) 'en route hospitality' is an initiative where owners can call in on others and stay on their drive for the night while plugged into electricity. It typifies the spirit of the organisation. Although we haven't stayed overnight anywhere we did call in on a couple in Middleton, near Manchester, for a chat and devoured a mountain of cake! Very civilized it was too. It's great actually because, like boating, we have something in common. I do like to go and pester a new neighbour when we pull up somewhere, whether in boat or van. You soon find out if they want to be left alone but with many, when you've got past the initial problems of broken fridges or misbehaving engines, most people have a story to tell and are quite prepared to share a glass of something unpleasant.

Part of the reason we're house hunting in this area is that our daughter Carly, partner and grandson live in nearby Uppermill. There are a number of routes into Uppermill, all of which involve scaling various large hills, bordering on mountains in fact. We're in the area that includes the Pennines and Derbyshire Peak District and our van is tested to its limits on the steep inclines. The A roads are like B roads, most bordered by dry stone walls which threaten to rip the side of the van off if you don't concentrate. There are also C roads and former pack-horse roads, one of which we took in error when the Sat Nav took us on the shortest route between two points. (Different to my boating navigation where I plotted the shortest distance between two pints.)

There were places along here where the walls were inches from each side of the van and we had to plough through overhanging foliage. When we finally emerged, having passed a dog kennels and cattery called Petsville (a place you might expect to see in an American C movie) we were covered in greenery and rather fraught.

Carly came to visit while we were at 'Steve's place'. She's driving around in a big white car / truck and Jan went to open the site gates as Carly approached down the hill. Waving madly to direct her into the gate, Jan was surprised when the car slowed but then kept going. She'd got the wrong car. The Indian lady driver was probably quite frightened by Jan's wild gesticulations and was likely weighing up whether to contact the police.

We visited Todmorden where I had both worked and spent my formative years in a variety of friendly hostelries. Included in these was the Golf Club where I'd spent many happy hours digging up the moors with a variety of steel implements and socialising in the 19th. Although it's (at least) fifteen years since I'd last played there, many members are still stalwarts of the town. When we called in at the (fairly) new Lidl I bumped into five people with whom I'd shared some happy times many years previously. It was like having a committee meeting, but amidst washing powder as opposed to the quiet of the golf club bar. The venue had changed but similar problems remained (bumpy greens, lack of members etc.) and I was reminded exactly why I came off the committee!

The exhaust is getting progressively worse. It's not a full-blown collapse yet, more of a growly fart, but when we came up behind three girls on ponies on a steep hill, their mounts were mightily alarmed. Feathering three tonnes of van on an ancient clutch is likely to lead to disaster but the riders finally came to a gateway where the horses set off across a field like a steeplechase. With manes flying and legs kicking about at all sorts of unlikely angles, they finally came to a halt at a distant wood. More friends we've made.

We have another cunning plan! Jan and Carly have decided they want to see more of one another, particularly now we have a grandson. This will mean more frequent visits. The whole ethos of our boat existence is to live simply and economically. We'd managed to get things pretty well sorted out – a reasonably priced, but really good, mooring in Belgium with the potential to travel south during the winters in the van and wild-camp on Mediterranean or Atlantic beaches. Now we're going to spend a few months in Northern England instead. Carly's house is not that big so there's no room at the Inn. This means organising accommodation. As I've said, staying with friends for anything longer than a few days can get fraught so the option is to stay in the camper. I'm not sure that this would be great during the winter so…….house sit!

We joined a House-Sit web site. This puts sitters and those needing one together. We concocted a 'profile' with a few photos and for £15 put ourselves 'out there'. Within 2 days we were contacted by a couple who live with a few miles of Carly. They have a nice house, a young cocker spaniel and a desire to visit their holiday home in Majorca. We went to meet them and, hey presto, we arranged to look after their house and hound for a fortnight.

What a joy it was too. They are a lovely couple who put their faith in us. We have no track record after all. The other potential complication was that we have a dog. He normally goes to stay with his 'Uncle John' when we need him to, but he was unavailable. So, the dogs had to have an initial meeting. Thankfully they got on like a house on fire (unfortunate phrase perhaps when looking after someone's expensive residence) and we were off. Our Tache was glad of the company and tolerated being pawed and clambered all over by the young spaniel. They charged round the house and garden and slept next to one another. We got lots of exercise too as we walked them separately to avoid the leads getting knotted as they zipped about. Hopefully we'll get the chance to go back there later and we have our first 'reference' for anyone else needing sitters.

While there a man walked past daily with his two dogs. He was a friendly chap who, as he put it, 'liked to make visitors feel welcome'. He's a lurcher expert (dogs that is, not someone who drinks too much) and being a former farmer had some interesting stories to tell. We chatted at length and one day brought us a dozen free-range eggs from his allotment. The day before we left Jan was chatting with him. She told him we didn't even know his name. In fact, I'd christened him Greengrass, after the character on Heartbeat, and Jan called him Bill Bailey because he resembled the comedian. Being a northern lad, he just laughed. Still don't know his name.

House-sitting eh? Isn't it peculiar the direction fate leads you?

Right, now I'm driving about with the back end of the exhaust in the driver's cab! It fell off on a steep hill right in front of a police car. I knew its condition was rather precarious and had tied it up with electrical flex. Consequently, when it came apart it clattered along under the van attached by the cable. Good job I'd 'repaired' it because the flex prevented the detached exhaust from bouncing through the police car's windscreen. The patrolman waved sympathetically as he passed and I collected my scrap. Actually, it's no noisier like this so I can delay a repair till I've finished some house-renovating jobs.

These jobs have become somewhat protracted. After having new roofs on both houses I've decided to completely re-build the bathroom in one and install a multi-fuel fire in the other, as part of damp-alleviation measures.

I was at the builders merchant picking up some slabs for the fireplace. Using the old camper as a works van raised a few eyebrows but I'd just finished loading up when, from behind me, very loudly.......

'FOR FUX ACHE' (pardon the language)

I turned to see a builder struggling to tie some ladders to the roof-rack of his rusty van. I asked him if he was OK. He was breathing heavily and muttering. He looked over and said, 'Who the bloody hell rings just when you're in the middle of tying a knot?!'

Good job the question was rhetorical as I really had no idea how to respond!

I'm really missing being on the boat but there is enough going on to keep us occupied and the northern banter keeps us amused.

One of the little houses we've bought is on Central Avenue, Littleborough.

It should be called Periphery Avenue because it's nowhere near the centre. It's on the edge, next to a lovely patch of land that, until a couple of weeks ago, was a football field. It's been transformed as part of the 'One Hundred Year Flood Defence Programme' into a big shallow hole, about the size of a football pitch, which is now full of mud. Very elderly natives have never seen a flood around here but that hasn't stopped the council digging up a sports ground on which generations of locals have safely played. According to one workman it has cost 'well in excess of six figures' – and they haven't started the landscaping yet. This vast sum is being spent while our wheelie bins overflow – now collected once every second month. Perhaps this explains why the previous incumbents had five wheelie bins – three of them for general rubbish. There can't be many cases like ours where the bins are worth more than the house.

Boy, is this different to the boat. When the gas runs out we just change a bottle. In our house we have a pre-payment gas meter. I've never come across one of these before and trying to get the gas turned on and transferred to our name has proved traumatic. This involved two initial trips to the local shop (where you can 'top up' the cards) where I bought a total of £26 credit. I inserted the card in the meter but it only registered one third of the amount each time. The problem is that the previous occupants had built up debts of over £100 and 70% of anything I put on the meter goes towards paying off somebody else's debt. The debt accrued because, despite no one using any gas as the house was empty, there is a daily standing charge. After hours on the phone to Npower (who supply both gas and electric) I was told that I had to visit another shop, four miles away, FIVE times on FIVE consecutive days and put £1 on the card each day. Only after this would the debt be discharged and the account transferred to our name. There are 'top-up' shops within walking distance but I have to use Mr Khan's Newsagents, which is recognized by NPower as a 'control point' for prepaid gas customers. I went early one morning before starting work on the other house. Not that early actually, about 7.30 AM. But Mr Khan's shop is in 'benefit city' so there's no point in him opening up early. He doesn't open till 9 so I had to return, yet again.

Because of this extraordinarily inefficient system, I will be invoicing NPower for a couple of gallons of diesel and five hours at £45 per hour for all the running around. Fat chance.

By no stretch of the imagination can I be called an expert when it comes to building, plumbing etc., but some of the things we've come across make me realize that there are proper amateurs out there. After we bought the boat I repaired or replaced numerous misbehaving things. There have been a few 'teething troubles' here too. The thermostatic shower didn't work because the hot and cold pipes had been plumbed in back to front. I solved this by turning the unit upside down and it now works fine. The blinds fell off in the lounge bay window. I feared that the bay roof was rotten but it's not. Nevertheless, it does need tarting up and I have ignored the first estimate of £700 to repair it. I will tackle it with a friend for about £50 – it actually cost £125, so all in all not too bad. We had damp problems on the outside wall of the lounge so we hacked a few bricks out and cleared the cavity which was full of rubble and causing a 'bridge' allowing the damp to penetrate inside. Hopefully, with the addition of a few ventilation bricks that's sorted that out. The chimney breast was damp both in the lounge and bedroom above. There was a leak somewhere up on the roof / chimney so we've had a new roof on, opened up the (big) fireplace that was full of rubble (and unventilated) and installed a multi-fuel fire. That should sort that lot out (although not cheaply!) The drain from the bathroom basin ran uphill – which is not ideal - so I've re-routed that and the water now actually flows outside. Costs to date – quite a lot. It will end up a bit more than quite a lot after having a new front door (old one rotten) and carpets throughout.

We're doing all this to try and improve our life while our comfortable old boat waits patiently in another world. We are living rather basically, camping in one room in effect while the rest of the house is in 'transition'. We're sleeping in the bench cushions from the camper. We don't have TV, just watch videos / DVD's, purchased from charity shops, on the laptop. We eat off trays on our laps and peer at the distant Dell. I did have one problem last Sunday – bacon and egg day. I'd had a busy week and decided to watch a film while eating breakfast (having put up all the dado rails, starting at 6.00 am). I suspect the reason why I couldn't turn off the Arabic subtitles on Top Gun was because I dropped my DVD in my egg yolk.

With the 'basics' done I've started further investigations. A friend once (unkindly) described my golf swing as being, 'like a sh*t-house door with a broken hinge'. Outside the back of the house, I opened a door (with a dicky hinge) on what I thought was a little shed and found – yes, an outside toilet! Presumably when these houses were built (around 1900) there would have been three bedrooms and folk would have used a tin bath in the kitchen and an outside loo. It's now 2 bedrooms (till we do some more conversions at a later date) and the bathroom is huge – bedroom size in fact. So, I had unearthed the original outside 'job-centre'. The door frame was completely rotten and it was amazing that the door had stayed in place at all. The loo itself is a high level jobby, with rusty workings and a broken toilet seat atop an ancient loo bowl – the kind of thing that would cost you a couple of hundred quid in a reclamation yard – an antique Royal Doulton. The reason I was ferreting about in here was that I believed this to be an ideal coal / wood store for our new fire. The idea had been to smash the toilet out and take it to the tip. Just to be on the safe side I checked the cistern and – it was full of water. I couldn't believe the thing was operational but I decided to give it a go. I pulled the rusty chain and lo and behold – water cascaded out the top of the cistern and drenched me. Actually, most came down the pipe and actually flushed the loo – then the cistern refilled! Looking like it hadn't been used in decades, it was amazing that the thing actually worked and it was a good job I had decided to check before just ripping the whole thing out. Even the float valve worked and water stopped coming into the cistern.

I bought an assortment of lumps of wood from the merchants to fashion a new door frame. I built the frame to fit the door but there were large gaps between the brick and wooden frame – so, expanding foam! I've not used this for many years so rather overdid it. Alarmingly the foam kept expanding (which it's supposed to) and it was in danger of filling the back yard and blocking off our neighbours back door before it finally stopped frothing.

Will all this effort put value on the house? Absolutely not!

I'm not sure how comfortable it will be to use the outside loo in the depths of winter but the whole unpleasant creation is certainly a talking point.

The front garden is only about 4 metres by 3 but it is like a jungle and contains a fair amount of cat poo. Until recently it was full of rubble bags, manky carpets and rotten wood ripped from the interior. We only have the old camper so decided to hire a van to take all the rubbish to the tip (in addition to a substantial pile from the other house).

The van-hire people didn't have anything below 2-metres that would fit under the barriers leading to the general public's skips, even their smallest was too high so the guy told me I could have a short wheelbase transit-type vehicle. When I arrived to pick the van up (I needed driving license, another proof of identity (passport), a bank statement that tallied with the address on a utility bill, a land line phone number and £42 payment for four hours and £200 deposit) they told me that they hadn't got a short van – nor had they a long one – so I ended up with an enormous thing with a hydraulic tail lift - overkill of the first degree. I was very nervous as any scratch or the smallest accident would be very costly – despite paying an insurance premium.

I'd hired the van for four hours and engaged the services of next door's 15-year-old lad to help me lump all the rubbish about and we managed it all with 15 minutes to spare.

So now we were just left with the jungle and cat poo. I dug all the grass up which went in to 16 bin bags. These I took to the tip in the camper and the garden was ready for a tonne of gravel – which I wheelbarrowed 50 metres from the nearest drop-off point. I bought a high quality, blue, imitation, porcelain-looking, plastic flowerpot from B & Q's 'clearance' section and put a motley looking palm tree in it – very tasteful.

Between the two houses we've got through 25-litres of paint and a few rolls of wallpaper – in addition to some wood stain, plenty of filler and loads of brushes and rollers. B & Q love me (or Buy and Queue as it's known).

So, in four months we've bought two houses and got them to a standard fit to rent out – and had a mini adventure in Van Wrinkle. Not bad, but I'd rather have been cruising the waterways of Belgium.

And what's Jan been doing you might ask?? Well, most of it actually!

Time to go Home

We've just returned to the boat after that protracted visit to the UK and have come to a decision that will radically change our loves once again. We've made a number of poor choices over the years, particularly financial, some with the heart rather than the head. Here's another poor one, we've decided to sell the boat and return to land full time. This is a 'head' decision and, although unpleasant, is the right one. For a variety of family / personal reasons we are going back to live in England. That means giving up the boat, and more importantly, the lifestyle. Perhaps the previous months battling about in the camper have given us a glimpse of what our leisure time may involve in the future, who knows. But it is all part of our voyage.

What it means is that we'll move into one of the houses. If we can rent the other out it will cover the basic costs, but in effect we're no better off.

The spring is winding down on our boating life. I, in particular, will be heartbroken to leave our beloved old boat. Yes, she's got wrinkles but boy has she been good to us over the years. We started boating in England nearly thirteen years ago. The excitement and nerves of that upheaval seems a click of the fingers away yet it's a period crammed with a lifetime of memories and wonderful experiences.

We are the types who try and find something in everything and I'm sure there will be new things to sate us in the times ahead. As I said to a friend recently, we're jumping into a hole, unsure of what we'll find at the bottom. Maybe Van Wrinkle will be down there, perhaps something else lurks in the dark. What we do know is that they can't take these years away, we'll always have them, always treasure them.

Just before we leave (so as not to end on a low) here are a few more happenings I related to my old friend...

Dear Nobby

Diksmuide, Flanders (doesn't matter if you forget now, we'll be home soon)

I look forward to seeing you. But not that much! It's a shame you never got the chance to come and see us on the continent. I know you curse your infirmity and, as you've kindly pointed out, the pictures I paint through my letters and other jottings offer very little insight into what actually must be a fascinating way of life. Thank you for your generous thoughts.

We could have lost the dog while Jan was out walking him the other day. Passing an open garage Tache dashed inside, after a cat or mouse. He was howling and frantically straining at the limit of his lead. He was spinning his wheels, running furiously on the spot, as Jan held firm on the other end. Then the automatic door started coming down! Jan was pulling one way, the dog the other. By the skin of her teeth Jan won the battle and Tache finally escaped just before the door clanged shut. She said that our little black dog's escape was like Tom Cruise rolling under a vault door at the last moment in Mission Impossible!

She also went to Lidl the other day. She goes at lunchtime when it's quieter. Not as quiet as they are in France where, during the four-hour lunch break, whole towns are virtually deserted, but it is still quieter nevertheless. I do point out to her that there are also fewer staff on duty, but it's a psychological thing if the store is largely empty. Anyhow, when she got to the till it was busy enough for there were two queues going – and she'd got in the slow lane. She turned to the Belgian lady behind her and said, 'Slow.'

'Slow.' The lady agreed

Jan pointed to the other queue. 'Quick.' she said.

'Quick,' said the lady.

Gesticulating at the two queues, Jan said, 'Slow, slow, quick, quick, slow.'

And the two of them started laughing and dancing a Cha Cha in the isle – much to the amusement of the other shoppers.

I don't know how she gets away with it. If I'd tried that I'd have been arrested.

See you soon

Fondly

Jo

The port here is really friendly and efficient – but it is not classed as residential. Not that we are residents as such as we spend time in the UK, but it means we can't have post delivered direct to the port. This means we have to have it sent via the post office. Not a real problem as it's only a kilometre away but a bit frustrating when you are waiting for something and the vagaries of the Belgian and UK postal services mean we have to pay repeat visits to see if something has arrived.

It's worse with parcels, as the following explains...

Our water pump, the one that shunts water around the boat from the main tanks, set on fire. Rather alarming all told and it's a fairly critical piece of kit it needs replacing as soon as possible. It's a good job I was around. You get used to all the noises on a boat and I went to investigate when the pump below started making a peculiar rumbling noise. The engine room was filling with smoke when I got there and I could see an orange glow through the mist. I managed to stop the fire by isolating the electricity but when the smoke began to clear it was obvious the pump was no more. So, I ordered one via the internet from a trusted supplier in the UK - and paid £30 extra for next day delivery via DHL's 'express' service. That was Thursday. On Friday afternoon I went to the post office - no pump. Likewise Saturday lunchtime. So, I went back to computer to try and find out what had gone amiss.

I decided to make a few notes for when I had a blazing row with someone...

...

Saturday afternoon

I'm very impressed with DHL's parcel tracking service.

It's very clear and informative giving a precise record of why my parcel hasn't arrived.

It tells me that it took only 11 hours from ordering and subsequent collection in Cambridge (England) to reach Brussels at 02:07 on Thursday morning where it was 'priority shifted' over to the 'delivery facility' (which turns out to be a shed near Ghent) by 07:04.

It also tells me that is has subsequently sat for 49 hours in the delivery facility awaiting 'next scheduled movement'!

I did try and ascertain the efficiency of their 'delivery facility' (with a view to requesting they induce labour) by phoning the DHL Express Customer Service Emergency Help Line. A very helpful electronic lady informed me that the office is currently closed – and would be till Monday – if it's not a public holiday!

So instead I requested a 'shipment notification' in the form of an email alert for the precise moment my parcel had rotted away in their shed.

I await the result with fevered anticipation.

Sunday. Had to collect water in a plastic tub from a tap on the pontoon for ablutions and cooking.

Monday. I had emailed the head of DHL Belgium on Saturday morning (as suggested on their web site) to have the matter of my non-delivery investigated.

On Monday morning I had two useless automated emails, one of them referring to a parcel sent from New Delhi to someone else in Belgium whose name was nothing like mine as it contained a few 'S's and a couple of 'V's! (My name is May)

Phoned customer services number in Belgium.

Very helpful lady told me the parcel hadn't been delivered – I pointed out that I was aware of that – in fact that was the reason for my phoning her!

She told me the Post Office isn't allowed to sign for couriered parcels – ah, new information.

'You'll have to collect it,' she said.

I pointed out that this wasn't exactly what I had expected from DHL's Express Delivery Service.

So, on this lady's instruction I drove 1.1 km to Diksmuide Post Office (just to check that our pump wasn't there - it wasn't), then a further 94.1 km to the DHL distribution depot near Ghent.

The depot is actually in a place called Nazareth. Perhaps the location is intentional – any delays can be blamed on the 'conservative' speed of a parcel being transported on the back of a donkey.

Apart from the short flight 5 days ago from the UK to Belgium, my return trip is the fastest my parcel has travelled in quite some time.

I returned to the boat to find an email from DHL telling me my parcel had been delivered!!!

The pump (Shurflo) is manufactured in Mexico but their European distribution centre is in Belgium, 150 km from where I sit!

I have ordered new pump as this one is obsolete.

So you see, not everything is straightforward. I guess it's partly my fault for not understanding the rules. It's a pity we have to go through a tortuous process to unravel the mysteries of a foreign land – we're not the first to get legged up and we won't be the last.

Diksmuide, Flanders

Dear Nobby

Here's a final memory of our time here. I know you are moved by the First World War so here is something we witnessed last October. The authorities called it a Light Show.

In October 1914 a front was established between German and allied forces (Belgian, French and British). It stretched from Nieuwpoort on the Flanders coast to Ploegsteert near the French border, where there is a memorial to the missing. The front was established following the Battle of the Yser in October 1914, when the Belgian army succeeded in stopping the German advance after months of retreat. The front stretched for some 85 kilometres and last night 8750 torchbearers stood along that line in remembrance of those who fought. We looked on from a privileged position on our boat across the river. It was an amazing sight as hundreds of people holding flaming torches lined the riverbank in both directions. As far as the eye could see, gradually diminishing lights paid flickering homage to those who fought one small struggle in a huge brutal war.

The Yser is the river upon which Diksmuide stands. It is one of three rivers that flow through Belgium but the only one that flows into the sea from Belgium itself. In addition to all the torches, symbolic bonfires were lit periodically along the Yser's banks including one here in Diksmuide and another in Ypres, 20 kilometres to the south.

The names of some 600,000 people who were killed on Belgian soil were projected onto the Ijzertoren (Ijzer Tower) in Diksmuide. In addition to the torchbearers, hundreds and hundreds of people came to watch and pay their respects.

In Ploegsteert, later in the evening, Princess Elizabeth, 13-year-old daughter of King Phillipe and Queen Mathilda of Belgium, read a piece she has written herself in front of 2000 people at the finale of the commemorations. Poignantly, she spoke from the point of view of the younger generation. Loosely translated, she said:

'One hundred years ago the Great War started. Thousands of soldiers say goodbye to their families to travel to the front. Violence, fear and hunger are their daily lot causing men, women and children to flee. Their houses, their schools, their towns being destroyed. We will remember all those victims who have fallen in our country and never forget. Even today, war shatters lives. Fathers, mothers, children suffering or separated. But in their misfortune, they also give us a lesson of courage and dignity. Will power in their eyes invites us to stand for a better world of justice and peace. It's up to us youngsters to hold our torch up high and form a light-front, like today.'

The Battle of the Yser raged between 18th and 31st October 2014. Time and time again the Belgians repulsed German attacks. An extraordinary fact is that more Germans were killed than the total number in the Belgian forces. Later in the month a decisive decision was made which prompted the end of the battle. On the 25th it was decided to open the sluices in Nieuwpoort and flood the river Yser and its associated canals. Water poured into the German trenches to the south-east of the Nieuwpoort-Diksmuide railway line. This prompted a frantic last effort from the enemy to gain dry ground, but they were denied, and with it opportunity for the Germans to advance towards Dunkirk and Calais.

Victory in this battle enabled Belgium the retain control of a small but crucial area and made a hero of Belgian King Albert - the Germans at this point occupied 95% of Belgian territory. There is a magnificent memorial to Albert in Nieuwpoort. Built in 1938, it has the hero King sitting on his horse within a circular monument made from bricks from the Ijzer valley. Below ground a new visitor centre and a museum was opened in 2014.

The railway embankment is now a cycle track but during the war it acted as a weir protecting the ground to the west from the flooding. As I cycle between Diksmuide and Nieuwpoort I can still see parts of the railway line and brick-built gun emplacements and shelters built during the war.

When we moved here we had no real idea of what had gone on. Sure, we knew there had been terrible fighting and of course Ypres is a name synonymous with The Great War, be we have slowly begun to appreciate the courage and sacrifice of the soldiers here in Flanders. We'll leave here with a new perspective. As with the wonderfully moving poppy display at the Tower of London, the commemorations in this region have ensured that we, and many others, will never forget.

We're on our way Nobby, put the kettle on.

Fondly

Jo

We're about to return and join a life once left behind, doing ordinary things paying ordinary (and expensive) bills. I'll have to return to work in order to pay the local council to fail to empty our bins.

We changed our way of life over twenty years ago. To be honest, at the time we thought Jan's days were numbered. We do feel blessed that she's still around and that we were gifted the time to share something magical.

Back home we'll love seeing friends, family and the grandchildren. Yes, there is another little one on the way. The smile on a child's face, in an instant and for as long as you'll allow it, renders any other problem irrelevant.

Boating, with its healthy outdoor life and constant shift of place and people, has kept us young and fit (relatively). But at the moment, while packing up and leaving the boat in good order, the thought of leaving the water and going back to live in a house feels like standing at my graveside between father time and the grim reaper.

Then, two emails arrive within a day of each other.

The first is the three-month scan of our new grandchild - clearly discernible, comfortable, waiting patiently. Magical.

The second an invitation to Christmas dinner. OK, it's three months away but somebody wants us.

It's time to go home.

Bonus Chapter 24

Vrouwe Johanna. Our three final days

Deluge and dolphins

Wednesday 8th March. Yes, the date is significant because it's still officially winter. Not many people voluntarily cruise their boat when there's a chance of wind and rain or snow and ice but we have no choice. We have to move Vrouwe Johanna from Diksmuide to Zelzate. Now, both of those names could be spelling mistakes, but they're not. Diksmuide is where we have moored our boat for the past two years. It's a linear port on the banks of the River Ijzer roughly fifteen kilometres inland from the Flandrian coastal town of Nieuwpoort. Zelzate is a dozen kilometres north of Ghent on the Ghent - Ternuezen Canal. There is a boatyard just out of town with a slipway where our boat will be hauled out of the water and surveyed. More importantly for us it's where we'll hand over our beloved boat to her new owner.

In many ways this trip is a lose lose. Firstly, it's not a pleasure trip, it's a necessity. We'll try and enjoy it of course but if we don't get the boat to the boatyard, we can't complete the sale.

Secondly, before we leave, we'll have to bring the boat back to life after being effectively mothballed for twelve months. It's a common-held belief that an unused boat is more likely to have technical problems than one used regularly, so I have brought a decent set of tools from the UK, just in case.

Thirdly we have to stop in the river current for diesel at the fuelling pontoon - after we've gone upriver where there's space to turn round that is. The current, after recent heavy rain, will be flowing with us - only about three kilometres an hour but enough to make things tricky on a narrow waterway.

Fourthly the first couple of hours of the trip will be down a fairly narrow, twisty river till we reach a lock and join the Nieuwpoort – Ostend Canal. We've never done this stretch before so we don't know what to expect. In fact, we've never done ANY of this route before so we're a bit nervous. We DO know that that there is a lift bridge to negotiate about half an hour into the trip so we have to phone ahead to alert the operator to raise the bridge for us. We hope that he (or she) is not asleep or in the toilet because we don't want to have to stop and wait in a current. Bringing the boat to a standstill should be OK but it's easy to get the boat a little off line. If that happens, the current can get a grip and swing you sideways – and we'd rather go through the narrow bridge nose first rather than get stuck sideways across it. Our boat weighs in the region of forty tonnes. The inertia is substantial and handling it in wind and current is not easy. In fact, you really need to get it right first time because it's very difficult to correct a cock-up, particularly to try and straighten it up if it gets sideways – even with the benefit of a 100-horsepower engine and strong bow-thruster.

Fifthly, the weather forecast is appalling – for today anyway. I won't go beyond fifthly because I've run out of fingers. My other hand is clutching my E-ciggy. I am taking a nerve-settling puff as a large log drifts past menacingly in the current.

So off we go. Hanging from our rear-view mirror is a silver dolphin – a charm on a black rubber chord. I've never been exactly sure why I bought it, but I did, in Leeds, West Yorkshire. I had it with me when we tackled the River Trent on our narrowboat. Back in 2006 we'd been looking out over the big river the evening before we set off. We were feeling nervous and insignificant gazing out at the wide, chocolate-muddy waterway when a small dolphin had swum upriver below our viewpoint on the high quay. I had my dolphin charm in my pocket as we cruised up the river and (daftly) believed it helped keep us safe. When we bought the barge in Holland I hung it in the wheelhouse and it has been there to this day.

We leave our mooring in Diksmuide for the final time and motor a kilometre upriver to turn round. It's not very wide so I remove a few riverside branches as the bow spins round in the current. Then, quite frankly, I make a bit of a mess of the fuel pontoon. I try to stop while heading down stream but as we try to secure the bow the current grabs us and the boat gets wedged sideways across the river, the front end tied to a barge and the rear stuck against the opposite bank. We extricate ourselves (with the help of the powerful bow-thruster), go down river, turn round again so we're facing into the current and approach the pontoon from downstream (which I should have done in the first place probably. Actually, there's no probably about it!). There isn't enough of a gap on the pontoon so we end up with our bow tied to the quay with the rear resting against the same barge that I'd assaulted a few minutes earlier. As we fuel up, rather upset with this bad start, it starts chucking it down.

We say goodbye to Pol, the harbourmaster who had looked after out boat for the previous couple of years while we'd periodically been away – full time away for the previous twelve months as we'd returned to live in the UK. He'd checked and topped up our batteries, put the heating on during cold snaps, cleared leaves and even removed spiders because he knew Jan had a pathological hatred of the things. Pol is one of the helpful people around the port who have made us welcome. 'You're a crazy man,' he would say, smiling every time I gave him a box of wine to say thank you.

We're off. The bridge operator was not on the toilet, the bridge was raised. The bridge is actually on a bend so we go through carefully, with enough power to maintain control but slow enough not to career sideways into the large wooden dolphins (bollards) that define the entrance / exit from each direction. Being flat-bottomed, our boat doesn't do corners all that well. There's no keel so it drifts sideways. The bridge operator sees us slew through the bridge and is on the phone about ten minutes later. We're in for another alarm.

'They have opened the river sluices,' he says, 'will you be alright turning right into the lock across the current?'

Allow me to explain.

Much of Flanders (as indeed The Netherlands) is below sea level, at least at high tide. Rivers, such as The Ijzer down which we are travelling, flow from inland, uplands towards the sea (obviously). The only way to release this inland water is for the authorities to open sluice gates at the 'mouth' of the river at low tide. We have seen this in winter when the river is in flood and a terrific amount of water is released through the sluices once they are opened up. At high tide the sluices are closed to prevent sea water flooding in. The river flow fluctuates depending on whether the sluices are open or not. Naturally the current is faster when they are open – as they are now.

So, what the phone call tells us is that we'll have to turn at right angles across this flow to enter the lock.

'The river is not as high as sometimes,' continues the bridge man from the safety of his lavatory, 'so they have only opened some of the sluices to give you more of a chance to make the turn. They will open the rest when you have passed through.' In effect the authorities are holding back some of the river Ijzer so we don't get sucked on to the sluices – which is pretty thoughtful.

So, we're heading for the unknown with our windscreen wiper (smearer) on full blast. To make things worse there is a 30 kph cross-wind – so all in all we're a bit agitated. As we approach the end of the river it opens out into a large basin. In the far left corner as we peer through the deluge is the narrow channel leading to the sluices, in the opposite corner is our lock, the entrance to which is delineated by two rows of wooden dolphins – which we can barely see through the driving rain. Another problem is that we can't open the windows so the wheelhouse windows steam up due to condensation.

Speed and drift are difficult to determine in poor visibility, particularly when the water is so disturbed by the wind, so both Jan and I have our eyes pinned to the windscreen in an attempt to spot the correct place to begin our turn. It's hard to know if the pull from the sluices affected us because (thankfully perhaps) the wind was howling from the opposite direction and each may have cancelled the other out. Whatever, we make the turn and scramble gratefully into the lock to be greeted by a lockkeeper who was both wet (having stood in the rain watching us) and smiling a smile that we took to be one of relief. Not half as relived as we are I can tell you.

Hereafter we'll be travelling on canals with no currents to muck us up.

We turn right out of the lock (it's still lashing down) onto the Nieuwpoort – Oostend Canal. After a series of lift bridges that fail to respond to my calling them on the VHF radio (so I have to telephone them instead) we moor for the night near the junction of this canal and the Ooostend – Brugges Canal. We've been travelling about five hours but it seems like a lifetime. Four days ago, I was laying hardboard sheets for a client in preparation for their new carpet. I reflect on what would I rather be doing. What I can tell you is that the buzz we get out of tackling a challenging day like this and coming through unscathed is not quite in the same league as scrabbling around on hands and knees bashing your thumb with a hammer.

Tomorrow we head for Bruges.

Day Two

This morning it's only drizzling but the medium-term forecast is encouraging. The breeze (much lighter today) is behind us so at least we can open the front windows to stop the wheelhouse steaming up. We pull into the oval-shaped lock at the junction of the Oostend – Bruges Canal and are immediately accosted by an official who tells us that our vignette (cruising licence) is out of date. He's actually trying to pull a fast one because it's not due for renewal until the 31st March and by then, with luck, we'll be back in the UK – me building a shed (or mending fences).

Despite flashing lights and the ringing of alarm bells we move not a centimetre forward or back (because were tied up) nor up or down (because the lock's sluice gates are choked with weed). The lock keeper leaves his control tower and hoiks weed out of the lock gates with a long pitchfork. After a twenty-minute delay we turn right (east) joining a much larger commercial waterway heading towards Bruges.

Much more pleasant this. The cloud soon breaks and a watery sun appears. There are a number of lift bridges, all of whom ignore my VHF calls. I'm beginning to think that there is a problem with it. I can hear other people chatting away but nobody responds to us.

We skirt beautiful Bruges' historic centre on a water ring road as church spires and ancient buildings pass by to our right. There are numerous bridges. Some, the type you typically see on English canals, look like a praying mantis, while others are quirkier. One is a white railing foot bridge whose bed remains horizontal as it swings left and up in an arc. It reminds me of a fair ground ride albeit one that doesn't complete a full circle. This one starts at 6 o'clock and stops and nine allowing us to pass below. Another is a road bridge where a section of road is attached to the thick end of two huge semi-circular 'cow horns', like two quarter circles. The horns roll backwards lifting the roadway. It's very peculiar seeing a tarmac road complete with directional markings perched high above the canal. Looking up from below as we pass the section of bridge resembles a giant waffle.

Eventually we arrive at another peculiar lock. This one is roughly circular and has three sets of gates. We'll go straight on and join the Bruges – Ghent Canal, a larger commercial waterway. The other gate is off to our left. I glean from our out-of-date map that it leads to a large drainage channel and subsequent sluice that can help remove inland water in times of flood. We needn't have worried about encountering large working boats because to this point, perhaps ten hours cruising, we haven't encountered a single moving boat of any sort. Perhaps they have more sense.

We're heading for a place called Beernem, roughly the half-way point of our journey where we'll stop for the night. It's a pleasant run and Jan takes time to catch up on some sleep after the anxious day yesterday.

We'd quite forgotten but we'd visited Beernem in our knackered old camper van two years previously but we recognize it as we pull in. There is a canal-side port, home to smaller cruiser-style boats, and a separate bar / restaurant which owns a six-van camping car stop where we had stayed on a trial run in our van.

The port made us welcome – 15 euros for the night and we had a beer in the bar. I left the lady an extra euro because I remembered that I'd borrowed a plastic lighter to light our camper oven and forgotten to return it. The lady remembered us but not the lighter. Am I too honest?

As we sit outside on the bar's terrace looking out over the canal and port, our dear old barge sits in the sunshine reminding us of the countless wonderful times we've had with her over the previous ten years or so. We're rather nostalgic because this is the last time we'll ever relax canal-side with our old friend.

The waterway widens out here to around a hundred metres and, despite encountering nothing previously, we now witness a constant stream of large commercial boats thundering by in each direction.

Day Three

Last day, with luck. Some big waterways ahead.

We have thirty kilometres to run to Ghent where we'll turn left onto the Ring-Vaart (water ring road) then turn left again (north) after a couple of kilometres onto the Ghent – Ternuezen Canal.

We meet a number of large boats (1000 tonnes plus) on the run in to Ghent but as we pass through Evergem Lock on the Ring-Vaart nothing quite prepares us for the scale of what we now face. Numerous boats, many well over 100-metres in length, weighing 2000 tonnes or more, ply their trade here. The waterway is concrete-sided and about fifty metres wide. The wash and swell from the big boats bounces us about, made worse as waves are reflected back from the banks. They are big buggers these boats and we have our hands full staying out of their way.

I can't wait to get off this waterway and turn north. At least I thought I couldn't wait. What we turn on to is in another league again. It is an enormous, industrial canal well over a hundred metres wide and home to sea-going ships – and I mean monsters. We're like an ant in the land of giants and to be frank it's really pretty frightening. The large two-thousand tonne things we thought were big are dwarfed by some of the stuff on here. Laden boats pass us carrying sand, coal, steel, containers and all sorts of other stuff that keeps Europe going. Seeing it briefly from this perspective makes me realize what is going on every day unbeknown to most people – it really is awe-inspiring.

As we turn left at the junction we look right into a giant cul-de-sac where waterside industry flourishes. Distribution hubs for oil and steel are the obvious ones but there are many other factories steaming, clattering and

BONUS CHAPTER 24

roaring in the distance. We're quickly forced to concentrate and look where we're going to avoid being squashed by working monsters that haven't time to bother with sightseers. Blimey!

We have about two hours to run down this waterway. Periodically large side-ports, perhaps a kilometre long by half wide, house more industry. Boats, both laden and unladen come charging out to join us on to the main waterway. The water in these side havens is being churned up so any disturbance hit us beam on and really rock us about. You wouldn't notice of course in a large vessel but in out shrimpy barge we are tossed about like a piece of flotsam. I am overawed and not ashamed to admit a bit scared. Jan is way out of her comfort zone here and looks genuinely terrified.

Boats passing from the opposite direction bounce us about but you can see them coming and prepare by turning into their wake, but boats that overtake us throw up waves that come at us from behind at an oblique angle. The result is that we go into a corkscrew motion until the water settles down again – until the next boat passes.

Then there are ferries that zip side to side across the canal. They carry cars, the odd lorry and foot passengers. Little swines they are that dodge between the traffic. They would be trashed in a collision with a large boat but we have to keep out of their way because even they are larger than us. It's all pretty stressful.

We pass boats moored on the bank which tower above us, huge things, four storeys tall. They are registered in the likes of Nassau or Helsinki and are often rather rusty with water discharging over the side from hosepipes. They are being loaded or offloaded by giant cranes, tonnes of sand or gravel in each massive scoop.

Then in the distance we see the biggest yet. In fact, through the haze, I initially mistook it for a white apartment block. It is a DFDS Seaways container ship, that looks brand new, and dwarfs anything else we've come across to date. It is huge but thankfully creeping along so slowly it doesn't cause a problem apart from the sheer intimidation factor. Far more uncomfortable is the wake caused by the empty cargo boat that thunders by between us and the giant resulting in another corkscrew.

Finally, we see the bridge that crosses the canal at Zelzate. It's shortly after this crossing that we will turn off into a small inlet and our boatyard. The bridge has three arches. The central one is for the monster ships and those at either side for more modest vessels – or tiddlers like us. The lady bridge keeper once again ignores my VHF call so I ask her on the telephone which arch I should pass under. She tells me dismissively, 'either the centre or the starboard, your choice.' The centre one is occupied by some rather big boats so we creep through the smaller right-hand channel. Once again we're rocked about as the churned-up water bounces and reflects of the banks and bridge piers.

At last, having passed another oil refinery, we turn right into the boat yard. It's a scrotty-looking place with a number of 40-metre slipways, two of which are occupied by rusty boats. There is also a selection of old containers that are probably storage units, a rather smarter storage shed and a small office block.

Made it!

'Moor up next to a boat called Amundsen,' said the boat yard owner when I had spoken to him last week, 'you'll find her on the right as you approach the slipways.'

Amundsen is actually one of the boats up on the slipway so we decided not to try and moor there, instead tied to a concrete jetty. The swell from ships passing by on the main waterway about fifty metres away still rocked us about but by comparison with battling them at close quarters for the previous two hours, this was relief indeed. I don't think we've ever been as glad to tie up to something solid and get out feet on terra firma.

As we sit and have a cuppa in the wheelhouse a monstrous cargo ship is towed down the waterway – two tugs pulling, one at the rear. The rear one facing backwards, presumably to slow the ship when necessary and help steer. As it creeps away to goodness knows where I ponder where we go from here, what our next adventure will be, will we have another adventure?

When you get through a day like this there is a sense of achievement, of something special shared. Jan and I have a hug and congratulate ourselves on being there for one another. We share a sigh and a smile that says, once

BONUS CHAPTER 24

again, we have experienced something pretty extraordinary together.

This has only been a three-day trip but an exciting one. Another paragraph or two we'll be able to look back on in our crinkly years. These have been the final seventy-two hours in a twelve-year adventure that started when we had our first narrowboat built in an industrial unit in Mold, North Wales and now ends with our dear old barge sitting in a scruffy boatyard in Northern Belgium awaiting her new custodian.

For us, it all ends here.

I put my little dolphin in my pocket and we walk away to rejoin another world.

About the Author

I wrote that last chapter three years after we'd finished boating. It's now five years on but as I re-read I can once again smell our dear old boat, hear her engine thump and growl.

Our boating years are a warm memory that floats forever in our past. We can delve in when things get tough and be cheered by any number of amazing memories. Just this afternoon we laughed together as I read out the 'hare in the supermarket' story.

Where would we be if we hadn't taken a crazy, wild decision all those years ago? Impossible to say. The boating life is not for everyone, at times it's not easy physically or emotionally. But for us the unpredictability and wonder of it all always outweighed any doubts we may have had. A dozen years of discovering what or who is round the next bend have, in the present, left us willing to try different things.

If nothing else, perhaps our adventures may inspire you to try something different.

We decided to have an adventure when Jan got so poorly she was told she probably wouldn't live to see the new Millennium. We can all enjoy cars, houses and chattels but we can also do without them. The one thing we can't do without is time and for us the clock ticked loud.

What's next? I did have an idea the other day. Jan is thinking about it. We always make decisions together as long as she agrees!

Jo lives in Lancashire with wife Jan and dog Tache.
　　He began writing monthly articles for a canal magazine in 2007. Following

an 'editorial misunderstanding', after which they parted company, Jo began to properly chronicle their travels.

They commissioned a bare shell and started fitting out their own narrowboat back in 2003. They did a second almost immediately because, as Jo says, the first one was a bit basic! They cruised many of the UK waterways on their second boat called 'M' after Jo's Godmother who died during the build.

They decided to expand their adventures so bought an old Dutch Barge in Holland and spent eight years on the continent cruising in Holland, Belgium and France.

Jo describes the memories chronicled in the 3 'At Large' books as being a huge warm memory on which they can draw during long winter evenings.

You can connect with me on:

- https://jomay.uk
- https://www.facebook.com/JoMayWriter/?ref=bookmarks

Also by Jo May

Three autobiographical boat books and two novels to date.

I enjoy writing. It's both a pleasure and a privilege to have done things worth writing about, it's also lovely that people enjoy them. One guy recently called Jan and I an inspiration. That is not something I would have anticipated when we took our first faltering steps twenty years ago.

A Narrowboat at Large
Jo and Jan May take the crazy, wonderful, potty, life-changing decision to live on a narrowboat. This first volume of the 'At Large' series spans four years as they begin a new life on the canals and rivers of the UK. The First question is why in the world would anyone want to do that? Well, here's Jo answer:

"Back in 1995, Jan was told by her oncologist that she probably wouldn't see the new millennium. Ever since those brutal words, time has been the most precious factor in her life. So together we set out to create a new normal. But why choose a life on the water? Jan can't swim, the dog hates it and I prefer beer. Financially we were afloat and we lived in a perfectly decent house until Jan came up with the zany idea of living on a boat.

We knew nothing about how narrowboats work or waterways lore, nor how we would cope being cooped up together – particularly when it's minus five and the nearest shop is miles away. We had a mountain to climb. You can only do that by using locks, and we'd never done a lock. A more accurate analogy is shooting the rapids, because our venture took on a life of it's own and we were washed down stream on a tide of enthusiasm and ignorance. We had to make it work or the people who had laughed and scoffed would be proved right – that we really were loopy. Well, make it work we did; we boated for twelve years. It was exciting, scary and marvellous and it quite possibly saved Jan's life."

A Barge at Large

A Barge at Large is Book Two of three in the 'At Large' series. It is a light-hearted, humorous account of what happened when Jo and Jan May arrived in Holland in 2007 and bought an old Dutch Barge. We follow their experiences on the inland waterways of Holland and France. But there is plenty for non-boaters too as Jo and Jan initially battle the Dutch language and discover culinary surprises such as Snert, an explosive pea and ham soup!

Their small barge was built in Groningen, northern Holland over 100 years ago and was in a sorry state when they bought her. In the early days there were times when they wondered what they'd done. The engine barely ran, the heating system didn't work and the rusty patches were growing like fungus on an old loaf.

Professional help was generally unaffordable so they learned to do things themselves. Over time they gradually improved things to the point where they could at least have lunch without an alarm going off.

Living on a barge is a life of compromise, less space yet more freedom, less cash but richer. 'There's no keeping up with the Jones'. If anyone starts being pompous we untie the ropes and go somewhere else.' Travelling on rivers, lakes and canals can be exciting or frightening and the story offers a unique perspective on an alternative way of life.

We discover the pleasures and quirks of new countries and the joy of meeting a wacky assortment of people. What's clear is that there's not really a typical boater, they are all different, having drifted into this watery existence from any number of directions. There are common problems such as misbehaving lavatories and dribbly windows but also shared delights such as wildlife, windmills and wine.

Operation Vegetable

Deep in the English countryside live a group of unlikely characters on their narrowboats.

Life at Watergrove Marina is carefree until a local landowner decides he wants to build luxury houses on the resident's vegetable plot. In an unaccustomed act of decisiveness, the boaters decide to form a committee to fight this scourge. Step forward Judy, a lady of physical substance, fierce determination and jocular disposition, who selflessly elects herself chairwoman.

H.Q. is the local pub and it's here that our ageing boaters raise a creaking battalion. Judy leads our disparate band into battle, implementing a plan code-named Operation Vegetable, a hare-brained scheme of doubtful focus. The boaters find help from an ageing rock star and a TV Gardening programme. Skirmish follows skirmish until one of the boaters is severely injured and the stakes are raised. Has the despotic landowner, a man of few morals, driven by power and greed, finally met his match? Will the boaters look like toothless turnips or can they cajole wobbly bodies, ideally suited to tea-drinking, to mount the barricades?

Or....have the boaters simply lost the plot?

A Bike at Large

A Bike at Large is the fourth book in Jo's *'At Large'* series.

When he was overtaken by a jogger on a borrowed mountain bike, Jo knew it was time for drastic action. Welcome to the world of a man in his 60s and his new e-bike.

His first injury occurred within one foot! Setting off for his first practice ride round a car park, he misjudged the width of the handlebars and scraped his hand on the cycle shop's stone wall.

'You'll go places you'll never have dreamed of,' said the shop owner. Prophetic words indeed. Eighteen hours later Jo was embedded in his neighbours hedge due to a clothing malfunction. Fortunately, before setting out he'd put his ego and self-esteem in the top drawer in the kitchen.

With the emergency ambulance on speed-dial, Jo climbs a steep learning curve on a series of mini adventures throughout the north of England, mercifully with a diminishing distance to injury ratio.

By calling his e-bike a 'Lifestyle Investment', it took his wife's mind off the cost. At the time she needed some new slippers, so it was a sensitive issue. Asked whether he was searching for eternal youth? 'Not really,' he said, 'more trying to keep out of my eternal hole in the ground.'

Fuelled by red wine and optimism, off he goes..........

Printed in Great Britain
by Amazon